Cultivating Intuition

Cultivating Intuition: An Introduction to Psychotherapy

PETER LOMAS, M.D.

JASON ARONSON INC.
Northvale, New Jersey
London

Production Editor: Judith D. Cohen

This book is set in 12 point Goudy by Lind Graphics of Upper Saddle River, New Jersey, and printed and bound by Haddon Craftsmen of Scranton, Pennsylvania.

Library of Congress Cataloging-in-Publication Data
Cultivating intuition : an introduction to psychotherapy / by Peter
  Lomas.
      p. cm.
    Includes bibliographical references index.
    ISBN 0-87668-528-9 (hard cover)
    1. Psychotherapy—Philosophy. 2. Psychotherapist and patient.
  3. Psychotherapy—Moral and ethical aspects.
      [DNLM: 1. Cognition. 2. Psychotherapy—methods. 3. Professional–
  Patient Relations.   WM 420 L839ca 1993]
  RC437.5.C85 1993
  616.89'14—dc20   93-9517

Manufactured in the United States of America. Jason Aronson Inc. offers books and cassettes. For information and catalog write to Jason Aronson Inc., 230 Livingston Street, Northvale, New Jersey 07647.

What a man believes may be ascertained, not from his creed, but from the assumptions on which he habitually acts.

—George Bernard Shaw

Contents

Chapter One

Introduction

The truth did not come to me suddenly.
It came quietly, circumspectly,
snuffling and whimpering, looking to
be let in many times before.
— Paul Scott

It is hard to justify the writing of a book. What has one to say? The vast majority of us can make little, if any, claim to originality. Yet if we write from the heart rather than merely mimic, what we say will not be quite the same as what anyone else could muster, and we can hope that this uniqueness may give our work a place.

Although we may not copy directly, we draw our inspiration from the work of others. We exist in a tradition, which informs our attitudes. If I look for the tradition that colors my own way of thinking, I find myself among those who are in acute conflict between two perspectives on the world. I know of no way of labeling these perspectives that would not be misleading, but *personal* and *impersonal* views of living are perhaps as good as any. Although crucially influenced by Freud—for it is he who has picked us up and placed us on the path of psychotherapy— I find that I am deeply and consistently moved by a desire to emphasize, in a way that psychoanalysis does not, the intrinsic worth of personal relationships. I refer to a belief that the value of relationships resides irreducibly in themselves despite the fact that they can be used in the interests of knowledge or for other specific purposes. Thus, the relationship between therapist and patient will be valuable in its own right and not simply as a vehicle for understanding the latter, and this value will be fruitful, since everything of value bears fruit.

The basic principles of our profession are embedded in ignorance. There is very little consensus about how we should live or how we can best help others to live. In certain areas we can expect to find much overt agreement in a society that purports to be civilized, for example, that it is a good thing to give food to the starving and housing and warmth to the sick, old, and penniless. But as soon as we move on to other issues we are in trouble. Is systematic education a good thing? We might not always think so, for much potential creativity in children has been stifled by rote learning and boring exegesis. How many Westerners would encourage their children to attend a school based on Islamic fundamentalism? How much harm is done by the deliberate falsification of history for political convenience?

And so with psychotherapy. There is little agreement on the desirable qualities of the finished product and little agreement on the means of bringing it about. No therapists are morally or ideologically neutral.

It is out of this mess—the mess of living—that we have to try to forge a practice that has sufficient coherence to merit terms such as a *discipline* or a *profession* and that can justify us in proclaiming that, as psychotherapists, we have something to offer to those in need and to those who wish to learn about our ways of healing.

The process of trying to help people unravel the confusions that block their ability to live fruitfully by being with them and talking to them is difficult to define. In giving it a name—*psychotherapy*—we thereby single it out from other activities of living, with the implication that it is a specialized procedure qualitatively different from our mode of behavior in other areas of life. Yet, as I hope to show in what follows, such an implication would be misleading. Therapy at its best is, I believe, the outcome of two people meeting regularly over a long period of time during which one of them, respecting the ordinary conventions of conversation and behavior, has tried to help the other to feel better and to lead a better life. Psychotherapy requires us to call on all the resources of understanding, intuition, and capacity to care, which are the bases of success in any important personal interaction. In short, the psychotherapist needs to use all of his or her experience of being with people. We could hardly expect less, for the patient is not coming to have her teeth fixed or her appendix removed but is bringing the damaged core of herself.

It will now be clear to the reader that in writing of psychotherapy, I shall not be describing a technique but will set down what pertains to one person's attempt to confront, understand, and help the basic state of being of another. The understanding of another may, of course, take time—perhaps a long time—to acquire, but that does not necessarily mean that the therapist need eschew a confrontation in the very first interview should he feel it is safe and relevant to do so. Much of the art of psychotherapy is learning when such a challenge can be made and what steps to take to bring about the favorable conditions for it to be made.

But the reader may say that although it is true that the patient does not come to have her teeth fixed, she may well bring a comparable problem. For instance, she may say, "I can't sleep at night," with the implication that she is not seeking a metamorphosis of her state of being but simply—and understandably—wants to sleep at night. Such a problem may be tackled in various ways: by drugs, hypnosis, relaxation techniques, behavior therapy, and so on—methods that can be used as alternatives to or in conjunction with the kind of therapy I have in mind. They differ from my approach, however, in that they are used with the assumption that the fundamental problem of the patient's failure to relate to the world need not be tackled head on.

It may be thought, too, that the approach I am speaking of is not appropriate for short-term work, in which, through sheer lack of time, one has to select and focus on one particular problem. But I believe this is not the case. Let me give an example.

A woman came to me in a state of extreme agitation. She could hardly contain herself to wait for the interview. A couple of days earlier she had been involved in a court proceeding and had, in her view, presented her case so badly that she had "blown it." She was now convinced that she would lose the case, which was central to her life, and could not bear to face the consequences.

During the course of a small number of sessions, we discussed the ways in which she had performed ineffectively in court and the possible reasons for her so doing. We even talked about strategies that might improve the situation at the next hearing. I felt rather like a coach or team manager, except that I felt able to question her motives for fighting the case. However, in the course of these discussions we explored her past relationships with her parents, the similarities between certain childhood experiences and the present dilemma, her attitude to parenthood and marriage and to living in general, her behavior in the room with me, and many matters that spontaneously arose without direct connection to the immediate source of her anguish. What occurred between us was not very different from that which takes place in long-term work. However, from time to time, both of us would, under the pressure of time, bring the focus back to the forthcoming hearing and the reasons for her miserable performance in the previous one. It seemed only a matter of common sense to do so. At no point did I feel I was using a short-term technique. Encounters of this kind are, of course, not always so straightforward. I was helped in this instance by the fact that a close friend of the patient had recommended me, and the patient therefore found it easy to trust me, which might not have been the case otherwise.

Despite my belief that psychotherapy is a much more ordinary and much less technical, specialized, or arcane undertaking than it is frequently thought to be, the approach I describe could reasonably be termed *psychoanalytical psychotherapy*. This suggestion needs a word of explanation.

Freud was foremost in getting two people into the same room to talk about the anguish of one of them without the intervention of religious dogma. It was an enormous achievement although approached in an extraordinarily roundabout way. Instead of talking about a person or self, he evolved a theory based on instincts and erotogenic zones and divided the psyche into three parts, and so on, in a dehumanizing and atomistic way. Much of this preoccupation can be explained in terms of his cultural background, and some of the damage has been repaired by his followers, notably the British object-relations school of thought. Be that as it may, it was Freud who taught us to confront the basic state of being of our patients. Moreover, psychoanalysis has introduced certain concepts that seem to me, and to so many others, to be of such outstanding use that it would be remarkably foolish to ignore or minimize their importance. It may be that in the future these specific ideas will not loom so large and will find their place less dramatically in the approach to patients, but now, in the shadow of genius, we need to take due note of them. This does not mean, of course, that in so doing we become Freudians, are required to do our work in the way that he recommended, or subscribe to his attitude to life, development theory, or system of psychopathology. And it does not mean that by the term psychoanalytical psychotherapy I refer to an inferior, watered-down version of a purer, more desirable and more rigorous procedure—namely, psychoanal-ysis—as is often assumed to be the case.

The concepts I have in mind can be summarized quite briefly. They involve the recognition that our childhood experiences remain with us and have a powerful effect on our present behavior in ways of which we are largely unaware and resistant to knowing about; that these early experiences tend to show themselves more clearly in the psychotherapist's office than in most areas of life, thereby offering a chance to understand and modify them; and that the therapist will be required to scruti-nize, at the deepest level, the reasons for his own responses to the patient and would therefore be well advised to submit himself to a therapeutic experience. These insights can so enrich our work that it would seem difficult to overestimate them. And yet in a sense we do. Overwhelmed by their power, we can easily come to rely on them to the neglect of the well-tried ways through which we have learned to relate beneficially to others. There are certain forms of behavior—spontaneity, encouragement, fun, tact, openness, humility, and so on—that most of us subscribe to as essential aspects of fruitful relationships but that can easily be eroded by a technical approach based on a specific theory. It is part of my purpose in this book to indicate ways in which this can happen.

This book is not intended to be a comprehensive account of psychoanalytic thought or a survey of the various methods and theories that have emerged since Freud. Rather, I hope to pass on to the reader what I myself have learned from such writings and, even more, from being in the room with patients. It is, therefore, a personal view. I hope that this does not imply an arrogant stance, for I take comfort in a belief expounded by several thinkers, notably Michael Polyani (1958), that all knowl-edge is personal.

One difficulty in writing a book that purports to be an

introduction is the kind of authority that the author claims for his statements. It is one thing to put one's ideas about therapy to whoever might choose to read them, saying, as it were, "This is my view. What do you think? Do you agree?" It is quite another to speak, as if one knows, to the uninitiated, "This is how psychotherapy should be done. Do it my way and you will be all right."

Psychotherapy is, of course, not like that. All therapists have their own way of working, based on what life, as well as training, has taught them about the way people tick and how we should behave toward each other. The style is not an epiphenomenon to a known and accepted method. The manner in which we greet a particular patient on a particular morning may color the whole session. At every moment, in every session, we have to improvise, living on our wits, hoping for the best, often lost and uncertain. Thus, I ask the reader to approach this book in the spirit of one entering a dialogue. I may at times—out of passion or in an attempt to make a point succinctly or to oppose a received view that I reject—write dogmatically. But I do not wish to convey that I possess a formula for therapy that can be followed as one might, for example, follow instructions on how to ride a bicycle.

Let me make an analogy. Imagine that I am a keen and experienced fell walker with a good knowledge of the English Lakeland, and that I wish to share my delights with others less familiar with the Lakes and warn them of possible hazards. I would describe walks and climbs that I had found rewarding, views that I thought worth the steep ascent, paths that looked deceptively easy, a conveniently placed pub that gave a warm welcome and a good meal, and so on. But I do not know the reader. Are you young or old? Are you sure-footed? What kind of view might move you to tears? Do you mind the rain? For all I know your idea of bliss may be to climb Sca Fell in the bitter cold, enshrouded in thick mist, or walk along Striding Edge by moonlight. I cannot tell you what to do. I can only hope that, among the ideas, anecdotes, memories, and such learning and wisdom that I may possess, something useful could be conveyed.

One of the many pitfalls in writing in detail about one's work is the difficulty of doing so without disrespect for the patient's privacy. At the risk of sounding pompous or sentimental, and using a word that can easily be misleading, I would say that there is something sacred about the therapeutic relationship. Patients have occasionally said to me, "I sometimes imagine you talking about me to colleagues, perhaps laughing about me. I would hate that."

Of course we all laugh at others behind their backs, even our loved ones. But there are certain experiences in which we have shown our nakedness to another, which are too precious to be spoken about casually, let alone ridiculed, and these can occur in therapy. Because of this fact, and because of the need in all cases of concealing the identity of the patient, much that might be illuminating to the reader cannot be said.

However, those who have read previous books of mine have sometimes told me that the descriptions of what took place in therapy were useful to them, and I have therefore continued to include such accounts even though I am aware that they are but a pale reflection of the reality.

When I was about to embark on the writing of this book I had a dream. I was about to give a lecture to a large audience. I had the script of the lecture in front of me. It had all been written out for me. On looking through it the previous day, I had felt quite easy and comfortable about it. All I had to do now was read it out. I took another look. The title was "Truth," but to my surprise and discomfort the text was meaningless. I realized that I could not now do what was expected of me. All I could do was to come clean. I decided to say, "This lecture is about truth, so I will be truthful to you. The text I've been given is meaningless, so I'm going to just tell you the truth, as I've learnt it, about what happens between people in psychotherapy." I felt somewhat daunted at having to say this.

Dreams often depict our conflicts in stark forms, but it is not always wise to take them too literally. I have not thrown away the script, which I assume to be the traditional way of describing psychotherapy, but I have tried to listen to the dream and to rely on my own personal experience when this appears to conflict with the known and accepted path, and to write about those areas of experience that seem to me of most importance.

Chapter Two

The Attributes of the Psychotherapist

"Understanding begins with the sensibility: we must have the experience before we attempt to explore the sources of the work itself."

—T. S. Eliot

When someone consults a psychotherapist of his own volition, he usually does so because he no longer believes that his problem can be helped either by his own efforts, by those around him, or by the ministrations of medicine and religion. However frail his remaining hope for help, it has not been entirely extinguished, and one of the immediate tasks of the therapist is to sustain this hope. To this end she may adopt two different measures.

First, she may simply convey to the patient any optimism and confidence that she herself possesses. She will not necessarily be explicit about this. The mere fact of listening attentively and with respect, and of taking the patient seriously and accepting him for therapy, may be enough to convey confidence.

Second, she may create as impressive a picture of her skill as she can muster. The caricature of such an attempt is the bearded, bespectacled, pin-striped psychoanalyst in his sumptuous suite with its portrait of Freud on the wall, exotic sculptures, and the couch with the Oriental rug. But those of us who practice in less salubrious surroundings, or work in the public sector, are not devoid of ways to impress the patient. We may have a high status in the medical or psychoanalytic profession, we may write books or papers, or we may, simply by our manner, try to convey great wisdom, learning, authority, and compassion.

The dangers of the second approach are obvious. We lose authenticity and we risk engendering the idealization that the patient, in his distress, is all too ready to acquire. Nevertheless, the therapist is understandably tempted to strain to impress, for she is asked to do more than is possible: to radically change the state of being of a person whose psyche may be crippled, and to have a degree of wisdom that only the gods possess. There is, however, a reason why the psychotherapist is in an easier position than it might seem. This is the setting of the meetings. Even before she has said a word, the psychotherapist is in a favorable position. She is a stranger to the patient and has had no previous relationship with him, which might impinge on the therapy in a distressful or confusing nature. The patient owes her no emotional debts; he is not in her power; he can assume that his shameful disclosures are less likely to upset or burden the therapist than they would his family. There are many paradoxes in this situation, some of which I discuss in detail later. One of them is that the patient needs the therapist to have the detachment of a stranger yet wishes to be understood in the most intimate way and indeed may yearn for a closeness the like of which he cannot find elsewhere. The handling of this dilemma is surely one of the many arts of psychotherapy.

Given that she will fall short—perhaps lamentably short—of an ideal helper, what qualities should the therapist display in the relationship? These, I believe, are primarily those that are required in ordinary living whenever, and in whatever way, we aim to facilitate the well-being and growth of another—in teaching, in social work, in bringing up children, and so forth. They are the qualities that most of us would probably list as the virtues of a good and mature person: strength, honesty, patience, humility, humor, shrewdness, a capacity to love, and so on. These are not, of course, capacities that the therapist can produce out of a hat any more than a man can add a cubit to his stature. She can only hope that she is not so lacking in them that she is a menace to her patients, and that such qualities as she possesses and the advantage of a quiet room in which she is free from the distractions and limitations of everyday life will enable her to give an attentive hearing to the plight of her patients and to feel a response to their intrinsic worth. The patient, however, is not likely to see it this way, for he has been referred to an "expert" who knows a method of curing him. And here we are faced with a difficult problem of terminology. In what sense is the psychotherapist an expert? In what way does she think of herself as being one?

WISDOM

The therapist has undergone an arduous training, has familiarized herself with the ideas of those who have pioneered this particular kind of task, and has acquired an unusual kind of experience that, one hopes, will help her to do the work; consequently, she is in a better position than the patient or the man in the street to predict and cope with some of the things that typically happen in the therapeutic encounter. Yet this expertise (if that is the right word) is far more limited than is generally thought, for the abilities that count most in the transaction are not ones that can be easily defined and are not limited to mere knowledge of psychological mechanisms and therapeutic techniques. The quality that is most needed is, I believe, best denoted by the word *wisdom*, whose dictionary meaning is "the capacity for judging rightly in matters relating to life and conduct." Unfortunately, the introduction of this concept is liable to bring conversation to an end, for what can one say about it that has not been said by those before us, in ways that we could not expect to better? It is, in fact, rather easier to describe what it is not. It is not, for example, adequately portrayed by a contemplative and immeasurably contained sage sitting comfortably in his chair giving forth measured responses, for on some occasions, with some patients, it may be more appropriate to dance around the room or cry. And perhaps it is only by recognizing its existence as a force and avoiding the idealization of its usurpers that we can make a place for it in our work, our training, and our thinking.

It would be immodest and rash for a therapist to proclaim, or believe, that she possessed more wisdom than her patient. What is required of her is that she be sufficiently wise to undertake the job, as a policeman on the beat should be in sufficiently good physical condition to chase after crooks but does not have to be a champion sprinter. There are many qualities that we would like our therapist to possess and that would give us confidence, for example, integrity, incisiveness, courage, strength, compassion, humility, warmth, tact, patience, and so on—the list is endless. But these are qualities that are usually considered desirable in other walks of life and, indeed, in simply living among people in everyday circumstances. Are there, however, qualities that, although not necessarily of greater importance than those I have mentioned, are of more specific relevance?

INTUITION

Much of the art of therapy depends on being able to place oneself within the experience of the other and to feel, in some measure, what it is like to be him. In this book, the word that I use for this capacity to empathize is *intuition*. Like many words, it has a checkered career, having sometimes been regarded as an attribute confined to angels, but I shall use it to mean simply "direct or immediate insight." To say this does not, I believe, imply that such ability is distinct from cognition or learning, but that it is achieved without a conscious awareness of a logical process or the application of theory. Intuition, therefore, should not be regarded as a magical gift that has nothing to do with thought or experience of life and that is intrinsically inexplicable. It is more likely that at the moment of gaining insight, we are quite unaware of the steps that led to our knowledge.

The salient features of intuition in relation to psychotherapy are, I believe, the following. First, it is a quality that some people possess to a degree that greatly enhances their capacity for the work; second, it is much more difficult to measure than, say, an aptitude for mathematics or a knowledge of history; and third, despite its somewhat enigmatic character, it can be helped by a learning process that brings additional experience and knowledge but does not attempt to diminish or replace it—in other words, it can be cultivated. And finally, it is an attribute of major significance in the selection and teaching of prospective therapists.

ENJOYMENT OF THERAPY

One of the qualifications for doing a job well is the capacity to enjoy it. The best psychotherapists are likely to be those for whom it is a vocation, who like talking to people about the things that are central to living, who are interested in the way the mind functions, and who wish to help others. Although the urge to heal must be essentially genuine, it does not follow that therapists are particularly saintly. As one might expect, much thought has been given by psychoanalysts to the obviously less worthy reasons for their choice of profession. Are they voyeurs? Do they have to compensate for repressed aggression? Although such factors may sometimes play a part, the most telling reason, and the one of which therapists are most aware, is, I believe, that they tend to grow up with a craving to heal a fault in themselves and their families, and that having failed in their primary object, they seek to do so vicariously.

Park (1992) recently interviewed a large number of psychotherapists of psychoanalytic orientation in an attempt to find out what kind of people they are and how they really behave with their patients. It is not a systematic study, but Park is an intelligent and sensitive interviewer, and his findings have the ring of truth. Psychotherapists, it would appear, are not sicker nor psychologically healthier than other people. They are dedicated to their work and act in a more spontaneous way than one would suspect from what is written in their learned journals. It is clear, however, that the occupation can be a grueling one. Several of those interviewed spoke of the difficulty of being constrained in one physical position – that of sitting in a chair – throughout the day. And the emotional impact of the work on them can take its toll. "There are patients," observed one informant, "who will give you a pain in the neck or make you pee blood or make you impotent." This is a rather picturesque way of putting it, but there is truth in the remark. I have at times found myself so anguished by the plight of a patient, so infuriated by his persistent defiance, so hurt by his rejection, or so undermined by his scorn that I have ended the session feeling drawn and empty and wondering how I could go on. And yet, when someone asked me, "How do you survive patients like me? Doesn't it exhaust you?" I found myself truthfully replying, "Yes, I sometimes feel that people ask more of me than I can give, but I wouldn't do another job for the world."

We are justified, I believe, in viewing our motives with

circumspection, for we are products of the Judeo-Christian civilization and are easily drawn into the heroic yet narcissistic attractions of pain and sacrifice. While reading through therapists' accounts of their work, one is struck by their emphasis on the sickness of the patient and the hard, long, and often back-breaking effort that has been maintained; and little mention is made of enjoyment and fun in the relationship. Even Winnicott, who had such a childlike sense of fun in conversation, surprisingly writes as if his work demanded such a degree of patience, stoicism, and subjugation of his own needs that it required a valiant effort beyond the ordinary. If it is really the case that we bring an undue degree of masochism to our work, perhaps we should consider whether in doing so we are really providing a good medium of growth for our patients.

THE PLACE OF THEORY

It is sometimes said, with regretful acceptance of an inevitability of life, that therapists start out with eagerness to heal, using their native intuition and ordinary human capacities, and do quite good work. Their brains, however, soon become befogged by theory, and it is not until later in their careers that the theory becomes absorbed into their unconscious, and they again do good work. Although there is some truth in the proposition, it is not one that should be embraced with complacency. Not all therapists escape the bewitchment of theory. And, if theory were not presented to students, as so often is the case, with such emphasis and in such a confusing way, they would not become so bemused by it in the first place. As with so many things it is a matter of emphasis. There is nothing intrinsically wrong in gathering information about a new situation before we meet it, provided that the new information does not prevent us from bringing to bear everything that we have gathered in life (including bits and pieces of theory) that may be useful.

I will risk an analogy. Imagine that while traveling in a lonely area you come upon a lost and helpless child. He speaks, but in a foreign tongue unknown to you. It would be of immense help to have a dictionary or other means of interpreting his words. But what matters even more crucially is the common sense, the compassion, the determination, and the experience of children's needs that you would bring to your effort to help him. And if you focused all of your attention on understanding the language and kept your nose in the dictionary, the child would benefit little.

This book is not, and cannot be, about wisdom, for I am neither Socrates nor Saint Francis of Assisi. The most to be expected is that I may be able to convey to a reader less familiar with psychotherapy than I some of the experiences he may expect to find in the undertaking, and to indicate some of the responses that, with the help of teachers, colleagues, and writers, I have found to be useful, hoping that this attempt does not diminish his confidence in his own natural intuition and wisdom.

Chapter Three

The Moral Stance
of Psychotherapy

What are days for?
Days are where we live.
They come, they wake us
Time and time over.
They are to be happy in:
Where could we live but days?

Ah, solving that question
Brings the priest and the doctor
In their long coats
Running over the fields.
                              —Philip Larkin

emotional one (MacMurray 1957). A passionately held attitude may well be the consequence of hard thinking based on experience, and what appear as factual certainties may prove to be strongly influenced by emotion. This kind of error reveals itself in the area of ethics when we make an absolute opposition between logical thought and moral attitude.

The way in which philosophy and science have affected each other's outlook in this matter is open to question, but there is no doubt that the attitude I describe is one that scientists uphold and cherish. The scientist firmly believes that his observations are—or, at least, should be—value free. In a limited sense this is justified. If something weighs 120 g, this is a matter of fact. Morality plays a part only if the scientist fiddles his experiment and notes it down as weighing 190 g. His requirement at this particular point in the experiment is to be competent and truthful. Even the scientist, however, does not exist in vitro, for his research will have moral consequences.

THE INEVITABILITY OF A MORAL STANCE

The principles of psychotherapy have their roots—by way of traditional medicine, psychiatry, psychology, and psychoanalysis—in the scientific attitude, and we need to ask whether this historical accident has led to a distorted conception of our calling. Psychotherapy is not, like science, an investigation into truth but an endeavor to heal. Although the attempt necessarily involves a search into the nature of anguish and ways in which this can be alleviated, the findings that emerge from this search serve as means to an end and are not the end itself. Should the therapist happen upon general insights into human nature and culture, these are fortunate by-products.

It then follows that the psychotherapist is more directly

involved in the practical matters of living than is the scientist. At every turn he is faced with questions of right and wrong and cannot avoid taking a moral stance. Let us consider a frequent predicament. A patient comes for help because he suffers from anxiety, depression, and various consequences of this state of mind, for example, insomnia and headaches. It becomes clear on talking to him that he is worried and unhappy about his marriage. His wife is as distressed as he is; there are continual arguments and progressive alienation. Where do we now locate the symptom? It would now appear to be in the marriage, and the question is already becoming more diffuse. The marriage is then explored and decisions have to be made. Has the therapist a right to suggest that the wife go for therapy or join her husband in a marriage guidance endeavor? Is the marriage a dead duck that is best ended? And what of the children? As for the patient, what kind of mess is *he* bringing to the marriage? His expressed misgiving about himself is that he feels he does not act as a proper man in relation to his wife, who he believes controls him. But what is a "proper man"? The man of the house who makes all the decisions and whose carpet slippers are warmed by the fire? A man who shows his virility by taking lovers? A man who doesn't cry? Or, simply, a human being, who shows courage, dignity, and compassion in his marriage and happens to be male? Therapist and patient are enmeshed, it seems, in the oldest question of all: "How should we live?" The therapist may try to bypass this question by focusing on the historical development of the patient's way of behaving, but the question will never go away.

The idea that the therapist has a neutral role whose function is merely to facilitate, clarify, and interpret is a fallacy comparable to that of the linguistic philosopher who restricts his activities to pointing out faulty logic. Certainly, the therapist will draw attention to inconsistencies, but he will select those areas of investigation that seem relevant to him. And here is the point of the problem (for who can decide what is relevant?): which of us knows what aspects of a person's life are of greatest importance—his sexual behavior, his marriage, his work, his spirituality, his ideology, his happiness . . . ?

The therapist is a child of his time and of his culture, and his views on living are all too fallible. Yet he cannot avoid taking a moral stance any more than he can pretend that he lacks a body and has no emotions. His very presence in the room declares an interest in healing. He is on the side of the angels. Even if he were to keep his mouth shut in the consulting room (and, of course, he can't), his writings and those of his colleagues implicitly reveal beliefs. His attitude to life saturates all that he says or does. His tone of voice, his manner, and the decor of his room reveal certain preferences even before he makes a response to the patient's dilemma. However much he tries to present his observations and interpretations as morally neutral, he will never quite succeed. Even if his wording or intonation do not betray him, his decision to intervene at some points rather than others shows the patient where his values lie. If, for example, my patient, who is an educated man, clearly reveals a sense of superiority over those less fortunate in this respect, I may take this as a natural assumption and say nothing, or, on the other hand, I may challenge it and talk about narcissism, idealization, overcompensation, and the like. Even such a simple statement as "I cooked dinner for the family" does not escape this net. Yet these values are rarely considered when we come to write our case histories or formulate our theories.

The reasons why therapists steer away from the moral aspect of their work go beyond the mistaken desire for a disinterested search for truth. First, the concept of goodness has been weakened by the decline of religion and undermined by Freud's revelations about our hypocritical efforts to conceal destructive aims. The word *moral* is now almost taboo. Second, many of those who seek help are already incapacitated by a neurotic sense of guilt, with the consequence that the therapist tends to avoid moral condemnation. And third, the therapist, unlike the priest, has no higher authority on which to base his moral beliefs and is therefore in no better position than the patient to know right from wrong. Yet, paradoxically, the patient hopes that the therapist can influence him to lead a more fruitful life, with the implication that he does indeed know how one should live. This daunting task is made a little easier by the recognition that we do not flinch from such an undertaking in ordinary life. If a friend asks us whether it would be wrong to act in a certain way, we usually give an opinion, however guarded and tentative it might be. What makes the therapist's position a more responsible one is that the patient is likely to attribute more authority to him than to a friend. And, although such an attribution is often undeserved, it can be justified by the fact that the facilitating situation, in which a thorough and relatively calm exploration of the reasons for the patient's behavior is possible, gives the therapist a chance to take a more understanding and compassionate judgment than, alas, is often possible in daily living (Lomas 1987).

If psychotherapy is removed from the sphere of morality, the practitioner is no longer engaged in healing a person but repairing a machine; an identifiable dysfunction has occurred that can be corrected by a technical measure. If it were a technique, the therapist could write out a formula and simply follow it. Despite variations of method, there would be a large measure of agreement about the general principles of treatment, for we would be in the realm of what Kuhn considers to be "normal science" (Kuhn 1970). Provided that he pursues his craft with authority and vigor and keeps within certain prescribed limits of behavior (provided, for example, that he does not rape, swindle, or slander his client), the technical expert's moral outlook on other aspects of life would be irrelevant. Because psychotherapy is not like that, because its subject matter is of a complexity beyond the reach of a general formula, the student is faced with a bewildering variety of principles, theories, and methods. Unlike, for example, the surgeon, the psychotherapist has no well-defined goal, for individuals elude any formula imposed upon them. The treatment is unrepeatable; as therapy unfolds, the aims change. The patient usually knows intuitively that this should be so and will not uncommonly protest that the therapist is not treating him in a "human" or spontaneous way, that he, the patient, is regarded as no more than a thing to be manipulated or a unit in a production line, and that the therapist's attitude is not real but a sort of professional bedside manner.

It is because the moral, philosophical, and political stance of the therapist matters that, for example, there exist psychotherapy groups that are organized by women for women, whose views on gender are at marked variance from those of Freud. Unless he is content to remain in a rigid and circumscribed mold, the psychotherapist cannot ignore these areas and will need to consider his outlook on life just as surely as he needs to question his adherence to any particular method or any theoretical school.

In the broadest sense, there is likely, for better or worse, to be a consensus of opinion among psychotherapists on certain values, that it is, for instance, desirable that people should be autonomous, coherent, truthful, and happy, and that it is the business of the practitioner to help them to be that way. Because most of us are middle-class intellectuals, we tend to look favorably on hard work, learning, artistic creativity, and worldly success; and because we have chosen to work in the "caring professions" we are likely to value an altruistic attitude rather highly. But such generalizations do not take us very far. Within these limits there is great variety. Psychotherapists come in all shapes and sizes, are strict or lenient, are dutiful citizens or unruly anarchists, enjoy hugging their patients or prefer them at arm's length, and so on. It is inconceivable that the huge differences in approach to life have no bearing on the way psychotherapy is conducted and taught. One's day-to-day work confirms this. Not uncommonly, patients have already had some experience of therapy, and indeed there have sometimes been several attempts at a cure. My own impression, gained from their reports of previous encounters, is that the way of being of the therapist and the moral attitude he took toward them have had a profound impact on the result. We are, however, still left with the question, "If the therapist's moral stance and his way of being are central to psychotherapy, where does method and technique come into it?"

TECHNIQUE

Although the word *technique*, is, as I have suggested, misleading if used to describe the nature of psychotherapy, there is no doubt that there exist tactics, strategies, and various ways of approaching the task of helping people that are thought to be useful by a consensus of practitioners who have a roughly similar framework of thinking. This is to be expected. There are usually widely accepted assumptions in a society at a certain period of time as to how a particular problem is best approached. It is not all left to spontaneity. And in our daily lives we adopt various measures and ploys for handling difficult personal relationships. What are called the techniques of psychotherapy (e.g., the interpretation of the patient's questions rather than the answering of them) seem to me to be a way of helping others in certain situations that is recommended by a person or group of people who have tried it and can support the advice by reason. If the source of the advice seems honorable and authoritative and the reasoning good, it is probably wise, to say the least, to give it some thought. But there is always the temptation, in aiming for the security of certainty and professional respectability, of following the method unthinkingly, thereby allowing it to dominate and corrupt the relationship. This is a matter to which I return when discussing the problem of ordinariness.

The artificial separation of function and morality creates the impression in the therapist's mind that he is faced with the choice between a pure ethical neutrality or a naive and unthinking exhortation to the patient to "pull himself together and get on with it." As Iris Murdoch (1970) puts it, "The vanishing of the philosophical self, together with confident filling in of the scientific self, helped in ethics to an inflated yet empty conception of the will . . ." (p. 76). I think that in practice, therapists do exhort their patients toward "better" behavior but surreptitiously and without allowing such actions into their theory. They do not treat patients like machines. Indeed, to imply that I, as a therapist, am more human, humane, caring, empathic, and loving than my colleagues would be the height of arrogance. But I believe that failure to recognize the fact that psychotherapy is a moral undertaking and that both parties have a responsible freedom of choice is liable to inhibit the personal relationship that is so vital to therapeutic success.

The dividing line between a moral and a functional action is a thin one. If a therapist concludes that his patient's narcissism is disabling (if, for example, it prevents him from earning a living), he may endeavor to understand it, possibly bearing in mind the classic formulations of Freud and the vast psychoanalytic literature on the subject. He may be able, for example, to show that the patient's fear of intrusion has led him to withdraw into a splendid, if painful, isolation. But if, on the other hand, he were to think in terms of vanity, he may consider the matter more a question of right or wrong attitudes to life. As an example of the latter, I will give a brief account of a discussion with a woman, a widow with a grown-up daughter, who talked to me about her wish for grandchildren.

"I would not want my daughter to miss the wonderful experience of having a child. But, for myself, the child would not be as important as the sense of continuity she would give me."

"It sounds as if you wish to continue making your mark even after you are not here in body."

"Yes, that's so."

"Do you think that perhaps making your mark is a substitute for fully living in the present?"

"It would be the next best thing I could think of."

I wasn't quite satisfied I'd made my point, so I went on:

"But isn't it narcissism? Isn't it the sense of doing well, of being noticed or known, rather than living well?"

As I asked this I was reflecting rather sadly and self-critically on my own wish to be remembered after death – not simply out of love (which is forgivable) but for recognition of some manifest, if modest, achievement that I might have accomplished (e.g., "Peter Lomas painted this beautiful picture. Come and look at it.").

My patient admitted that she did indeed feel this was true of her, and we went on to discuss the issue. She quoted extracts from the Bible (not out of any religious conviction but because the passages had had an impact on her): "Consider the lilies of the field, how they grow . . ." and "Lay not up for yourselves treasures upon earth, where moth and rust doth corrupt." I feel that this discussion, in which we were both open about our values, helped to elucidate her problem and caused her to reflect on her attitude to life.

Chapter Four

The Analytic Attitude

Mr. Elliot was rational, discrete, polished, but he was not open. There was never any burst of feeling, any warmth of indignation or delight, at the evil or good of others. This, to Anne, was a decided imperfection.

—Jane Austen

Having abandoned hypnosis, Freud sought an alternative method of discovering what lay behind consciousness. The basic rule upon which he alighted recommended that the patient should say everything that came into her head without making any attempt at selection or censorship. In order that this task be more readily accomplished, external stimuli were reduced to a minimum; there were to be no distractions. The patient lay on the couch, unable to see the analyst who stayed quietly in the background. There is no doubt that such an approach can help to reach the objective that Freud intended. I will give an example.

A woman who had been coming to me for two years felt that she had now met up with a block. Although she had hitherto resisted the idea of lying on the couch, I now suggested this. With trepidation she did so. For a few minutes she was silent. Then she said, "I feel terrible. I feel utterly alone. I've never felt like this, at least not since a child. There's nothing. It's desolate. You have disappeared." Then she remembered how, in her country, small children were swaddled and kept in a box with high sides most of the time, unable to see anyone. She found the present experience almost unbearable but stuck it out and continued to use the couch. At one point she said, "You know, I couldn't have done this earlier in the therapy. I would have gone mad." (I doubt if her belief in a catastrophic outcome was, in fact, justified, for her defenses would have ensured that the feelings remained repressed.)

This is one of many possible examples that suggest that Freud's method can be of major importance in helping a patient to reexperience the past, although it does not necessarily follow that this procedure should be used as a routine. It is a method that, as Freud maintained, involves a degree of frustration. There is little for the patient to hang on to; her strategies for getting by in the world, the disguising of painful and embarrassing feelings by conventional social moves, the manufacture of purpose to give meaning to an empty existence, and the good works that justify her existence have been removed. She may have to say, "I don't know what I want. I don't know how to live. I don't know how to be." And the predicament is there before us. She may, of course, elude such insight by focusing, for example, on performing well as a patient, asking, "Tell me how to do this." But sooner or later, in successful therapy, the ploys and distractions will be shown to be a means of escape. This creative deprivation is not unlike (although somewhat less enigmatic than) that to which the Zen master subjects his pupil when asked to reveal the way to wisdom.

Despite the telling arguments in favor of this approach, it is not without its dangers and disadvantages, some of which I am concerned with in this book. But even among those therapists who regard the method to be unnecessarily rigid and who allow themselves more flexibility in practice (indeed, Freud himself gave up his original insistence that the patient close her eyes), there remains a widespread adherence to the principles that informed those measures. We must, therefore, consider what is commonly referred to as the *analytic attitude*.

THE MERIT OF THE ANALYTIC ATTITUDE

The analytic attitude is best thought of as a certain frame of mind in which the therapist approaches his patient. He listens and watches. He is attentive in a way that is unusual in daily living: he respects the patient's need for room to think; he tries to minimize irrelevancies; and he looks for meanings and responses beyond the obvious. He does not rush in with the first thing that comes into his head. In the kind of setting that Winnicott calls *a medium for growth* or *a facilitating environment*, experiences can occur for which there has been no space hitherto.

The difference between the therapeutic milieu and that of daily living is not, of course, absolute. In ordinary life, we do not always plunge unthinkingly into a conversation, spilling out whatever happens to be at the forefront of our minds. We are, in varying degrees, selective and reflective. When our primary concern is the well-being of the other, we may withhold for reasons similar to those of the therapist: we may not say what is in our minds if it seems irrelevant or intrusive at that moment, or if it would be misleading or hurtful. Such a reserve is usually spoken of as consideration or tact. It is authentic. Although it may involve a sacrifice of certain immediate truths that could have been revealed, we are not necessarily out to manipulate, confuse, score over, patronize, or bring harm to the other. It can be seen, therefore, that the analytic attitude, however much it may have derived from Freud's theories of psychopathology and technique, is in fact an intensified form of the way we behave at times in ordinary life when we are confronted by someone who wishes to tell us about a problem.

A cogent and authoritative version of the analytic attitude has been stated by Schafer (1983). "The analyst," he writes, "remains neutral in relation to every aspect of the material presented by the analysand" (p. 5). He should avoid moral judgments. His job is to interpret, and he does not "respond in kind" to the patient's overtones: "By not responding in kind I mean, for example, not meeting love with love or rejection or exploitation; not meeting anger with retaliation or self-justification or appeasement; and not meeting confidences with thanks or with self-revelations of one's own" (p. 9). Thus, his ideal is "to rely so far as possible on interpretation and careful preparation for interpretation through confrontation and clarification." "This ideal," Schafer continues, "will appear to be inhumanly rigid, exploitative, authoritarian, or unsupportive only to those who reject the general guidelines of psychoanalytic understanding and so do not appreciate the benefits ultimately to be derived from the analyst's consistently maintaining the analytic attitude" (p. 9). The analysis should "take place in a context of unabashed, unfussy, untheatrical, and unhectoring human relatedness," but reassurance is to be strictly avoided at all costs.

The chief merit of the analytic attitude, therefore, is that it encourages the patient to talk as freely as possible and enables the analyst to pay attention without distraction. A crucial element in the patient's ability to express himself openly is freedom from guilt. Many of those who seek therapy are, consciously or unconsciously, wracked by guilt. Although, as Melanie Klein so fruitfully maintains, this is often the consequence of destructive fantasies toward the parents and a consequent urge to make reparation, it would appear that children often grow up under the oppressive weight of a need to spare their unhappy, insecure parents from any anxiety and grief. For this reason, a therapeutic stance that eschews retaliation, condemnation, or heavy criticism is likely to be helpful.

In a paper on free will, Symington (1990) formulates the question of the analyst's reticence in an interesting manner. He contrasts two different ways of relating to what the patient brings—the *reactive* and the *responsive*—and gives an account of an occasion when he managed to change his attitude in favor of the responsive. He recounts the bruising words of a patient who claims that he is of no help to her, but that she has found someone else "who is really sympathetic to women." He writes:

> my inner anatomy was a surging millrace and also a fury at her insinuations. I was about to point out her destructive attacks on me and her attempt to denigrate all the work I did with her but I held it. I did not hold it easily, there was a tug of war inside me: one side was saying "point out her denigration" while the other side was saying "hold it." . . .
>
> The "hold it" side won and then calmness began to come over me and then in that state of calm another thought came forth. I said to her quite calmly that she was letting me know that she was now able to communicate with people other than me outside the consulting room. [p. 101]

Drawing on the ideas of Bion, Symington maintains that the reactive mode is based on anxiety that has not been contained, whereas in the responsive mode, he had transcended the anxiety and was able to think his own thoughts. The point that Symington makes—indeed, the point of his paper—is that it is only when we can withstand and contain the bombardment of the other's words and actions that we can think our own thoughts and make a free statement. This statement is therefore a consequence of reflection. When we react, we merely bully and do not reach the center of the other. When we respond, we have transcended the immediate impressions upon us, and they have "become servants to our personal center."

THE AMBIGUOUS NATURE OF SPONTANEITY

It would appear that a spontaneous statement—an authentic, vital, and genuine one—is likely to be of a responsive kind. Yet many writers, including myself, have criticized the lack of spontaneity of a very considered, reflective, technical approach to patients, caricatured by the analyst who sits behind his patient and occasionally grunts or makes measured, unemotional interpretations—who manifests a daunting purity and is, in the common meaning of the word, unresponsive. How can this apparent paradox be resolved?

The difficulty arises from ambiguity over the word *spontaneous* and the resultant confusion between behavior that is precipitate and that which is not. To make a spontaneous response, we need to be free from both the pressure to react unthinkingly and the pressure to restrain ourselves unduly— pressures that may emanate from either our own psyche or the outer world. In therapy, we have to tread a path that is dictated by neither the bombardment of the patient's coercive powers nor the inhibitions of our own caution or rigid technique. There is, I believe, a world of difference between a reticence that is inviolate and one that can be bridged; and we have to consider the relative merits of both approaches. Because therapists vary in the degree to which they adhere to a systematic reticence, this is a difficult question to address. No one enjoys being thought either rigid or sloppy, and we are inclined to think of ourselves as having managed to get it just right; and "just right" for one therapist may be quite different for another. The word *spontaneous* has a favorable moral connotation, calling to mind a warm, generous person who speaks and acts from the heart— someone who is authentic. It would seem, however, that what is significant in relation to the word is whether we are referring to an individual action or a general tendency. The spontaneous person is so constituted that he acts in a flexible way, whether or not he decides at one particular time to respond with a word, a kiss, or silence. He is open to the other but not necessarily precipitate. His response is appropriate to the moment rather than a reaction that depends on habit, rule, technique, formality, or personal defense. A quick answer, or, by contrast, a reflective pause, may be different manifestations of one overall attitude of mind that is neither precipitate nor withdrawn. As an example of this in practice, I will describe the degree of the reserve with which, rightly or wrongly, I respond to a patient.

Glenys came for her psychotherapy session, having traveled a long distance in the morning fog. I had wondered how she was faring and was surprised that she arrived on time. However, I made no mention of the journey; nor did she. If the situation had been one of ordinary friendship it would, I think, have seemed inconsiderate of me and unduly reticent of her to have ignored the fact of the fog. But it was not ordinary friendship; we were meeting for a specific purpose. What was important to her at that moment may well have transcended the problems of the journey. I did not know what was most pressing for her, and I did not want to disturb or distract from whatever it might be. I knew from my memory of the previous session that it was likely to be intense and intimate. Although I gave her a smile and said "Hello," my response was, to an extent, passive, muted, and unspontaneous.

What passed between Glenys and me needs to be understood in the light of the relationship as a whole. She knows that if she had said, "I've had a terrible journey" and "Did you worry about me?" I would have shown interest in her tribulations and answered her question. However, once Glenys sat down it became only too clear that the weather conditions were the least of her problems.

"I feel miserable," she began. "I am such a horrible person. I can't get on with anyone and would be better on a desert island."

I said, "This isn't all of you. You love as well. I think I know how you feel. Sometimes at 3 A.M. I become aware of what a narcissistic, ambitious, egotistical person I am, and I despair of myself. But I know it's not all of me. You're forgetting the loving part of yourself. I don't think you're a horrible person. Quite the reverse."

"I believe you. I know you wouldn't lie to me."

In this interchange, I responded in what appears to be an ordinary, commonsense way, and I would like to compare this with something that had occurred in the previous session.

Glenys had told me a dream in which she was half dead and lying in a grave. Fierce dogs had savaged her, tearing the flesh off her bones. In the course of discussing the dream, I said, "The night you had the dream followed directly on the session when I had a large plaster on my nose. Yet you never commented on this, and I was surprised."

"I didn't want to intrude on you."

"Did you have any fantasy about the nose?"

Glenys looked abashed and gave a wry smile. "Yes. I thought you'd been bitten by a dog."

We both laughed because we had a good idea what this is about, for Glenys has quite bloodcurdling fantasies of eating me and tearing at me. On the particular day in question, she had ended the session by saying, "I don't want to go. I want to stay here all day and drink warm milk."

It may be thought that my implicit interpretation in the previous session was of a quite different kind from the common-sense reaction described above, that it was technical as opposed to spontaneous. But is this so? There was, perhaps, no more calculation in the second than in the first. My commonsense reaction was not, I hope, unreflective, even though it came quickly. It is likely that somewhere at the back of my mind was an assessment of Glenys's need for reassurance and the useful-ness, at that point, of giving it. Moreover, the second response, which was influenced by a particular piece of theory (that we often deny our own aggression and displace it onto another person or agency), does not, I believe, invalidate its spontaneity. Our ordinary reactions are influenced by insights that we happen to have gained during our lives from whatever source. And the fact that, like many psychotherapists, I find the insights of Freud to be of quite exceptional value, does not necessarily alter the case. Freud's theories (and, indeed, all the experience gained during the course of learning and practicing psychotherapy) enable us to increase the repertoire of our available responses to the patient. We come to know of specific and surprising psychic mechanisms, and we learn that we do not have to react to our patients according to social convention or personal habit. We must also remember, however, that the conventions of psychotherapeutic technique offer a comparable threat to our capacity to respond spontaneously.

Absolute spontaneity is elusive and probably unattainable. In all we do and think, there is a guiding force derived from historical, social, and personal factors, which limits the possibilities open to us. Thus, spontaneity is a matter of degree. If a patient were to look at one of his therapist's pictures and say, "I like that," the therapist might make an immediate psychoanalytical interpretation ("It has the contours of a breast, hasn't it?"), or, hoping for more material, "Tell me why you like it", or, encouraging his self-image, "I'd love to know what you have to say about it. I value your judgment." Or, finally, without any underlying aim of helping the patient therapeutically, he may say, "Oh. I'm glad you like it. The colors are terrific, aren't they?" In this last example, the therapist has set aside or forgotten the purpose of the visit and is enjoying the patient's company. He has freed himself from his task. There will be constraints on his freedom even in these moments, but a therapy that eschews such experiences sacrifices the kind of spontaneity that vitalizes a relationship.

Although what is good for either the therapist or the patient is likely to bring benefit to both, this is not always the case. Even if the analytic attitude were to meet the patient's needs ideally, the therapist will be able to maintain it with grace and humanity only if his own needs are met to a certain degree. A continuous application of restraint is, in ordinary life, difficult to achieve without undue cost, and, even in the favorable set-up of the consulting room, this is also the case in psychotherapy. How does the practitioner deal with this predicament? He may seek therapy himself to assuage his pains. He may suffer somatically, or his relatives or friends may suffer. Or he may unconsciously deprive the patient of his warmth, rationalizing his retaliatory withholding in the name of technique.

There is no ideal attitude to take toward a patient any more than there is an ideal attitude to take toward a wife, husband, or lover. We can say with confidence that the analytic attitude is a useful guideline to keep in mind, and that we should recommend it in rather the same spirit that we would advise a hiker to wear sturdy and comfortable footwear but would be unwise to insist that all hikers wear boots of a particular design.

Chapter Five

The Nature of Interpretation

The history of interpretation, the skills by which we keep alive in our minds the light and dark of past literature and past humanity, is to an incalculable extent a history of error.

—Frank Kermode

When we interpret, we expound or elaborate the meaning of something, often by placing it in a different context. By means of interpretation, our behavior is seen in a new light, and we become aware of significances that were previously hidden. We hope that the new perspective will increase our insight, but it will do this only if it adds to our vision without destroying what was there before and if the fresh insight is superior to the old one. Those who come for psychotherapy are often confused and restricted in their vision and will be helped if we can find meaning in what appears to be chaos or extend the meaning of limited thoughts by showing that there are contexts in which their words have other meanings.

The contribution of Freud to this subject lay in his statement that the relevant context of a thought or feeling is often rendered inaccessible to people by their anxious determination to remain unaware of it, that it shows itself only indirectly, in mistakes, dreams, fantasies, and symptoms, and that the analyst needs to understand this hidden language in order to make meaning of the patient's confused words and actions. Furthermore, exploration of these unconscious phenomena showed that they are primarily concerned with childhood urges, memories, and fears.

Just as we can learn to speak without a formal knowledge of grammar and sing without a mastery of musical theory, so we can, with a little help, come to understand the way dreams use symbolism. The elements of Freud's theory can be learned quite quickly. The main feature is that, in dreams and comparable phenomena, one image may stand for another or several ideas can be condensed into one image. By means of his theory, Freud prevailed upon us to take dreams seriously and to look at them as a different and more fluid representation of our experience. In actual practice, the facility with which people are able to understand dreams does not seem to depend on their knowledge of theory but on their intellectual flexibility. I will now give an example of the way in which a dream may throw some light on a patient's problem.

Alex suffered from an intrusive and persistent fascination with men of a certain kind of physical appearance and social status. If such a man came within her sight, she became extremely agitated and preoccupied, pursued him in order to win him, yet should he appear to respond to her advances, she was quite unable to believe that his behavior was in any way genuine. During the therapy, we had explored the childhood antecedents of this obsession.

One night Alex dreamed that she wished she were dead. The next night she had the following dream:

"I was in the village where I grew up, in the garden of a big house, with the children I used to know. It was dark. You were there. You led me to a hole in the ground and said, 'You must see this. It's important for your therapy.' I was terrified and crying. I said, 'I can't look in! I can't face it.' You put your arm round me and insisted that I look. I could see now that the hole was a grave, and in it there was a coffin. It was not quite adult size."

Since the death of her young child, Alex had had many dreams about this tragedy, but she had, I believed, painfully and courageously accepted his death, and I did not feel that the dream was simply about this loss. One clue to the dream seemed to lie in the size of the coffin, which suggested that it contained a teenager of 15 or 16. I asked her what she could remember of herself at that age and whether something might have died in her then.

Alex then told me of a traumatic love affair with an older man when she was 16. She worshipped him and each day performed slimming exercises in order to attract him, but eventually he rejected her. All she wanted to do afterwards was to sleep, and she became so ill that there were fears for her life. It seems likely that she was struggling at that time with a powerful wish to die.

Alex had been coming to me for over a year and was a very open person. We had learned, up to a point, the childhood origins of her present problems, but until now her adolescent years had remained unexplored. This dream led us to them. All that was needed was to understand the simple symbolism of the dream: the death that was depicted referred to the dreamer's state of mind. I do not, however, wish to make it sound all too easy. The meanings of any dream seem endless, and I cannot pretend to have elucidated more than one element in this one—but it was a helpful one to us. Moreover, Alex's dreams were usually illuminating. Sadly, this is by no means always the case.

A dream will sometimes depict not only what is being repressed but the urge to keep it in repression. A man dreamed the following:

"I was at the front door of my house when the postman appeared with some letters. He was unfamiliar to me, a youngish man with a contorted face who was trying desperately hard to find words to convey a message but was incoherent with anguish. With a mixture of supplication and anger, he pushed wildly at my chest and pinned me against the door. Then he withdrew but turned round as he went and gave me a hateful stare. I felt uneasy at my privileged position in my safe house. Later, I saw him behaving in a similar manner toward someone in the road. I was relieved. I thought, 'He's nothing to do with me. It's not personal.' "

The patient felt that the postman represented himself. An association to the dream confirmed this idea by referring to an incident in his life when he had felt utterly crushed and rejected by someone despite having pleaded in a painfully humiliating way. It would appear that the message he was reluctant to receive was the existence of a disabled, anguished, and underprivileged self clamoring to be given recognition.

THE ART OF INTERPRETATION

Wherein lies the art of interpretation?

There is no doubt that a facility for translating unconscious symbolism is important, and that it grows with practice, but there are equally important gifts. A useful interpretation depends on common sense, tact, a sense of timing, intuition, and many other factors that are difficult to formulate but add up to a capacity to judge whether, when, and how the interpretation is best made.

There would seem to be two ways in which to seek the meaning of a dream. First, as advocated by Freud, one asks the patient to give her associations to the various images in the dream and painstakingly puts the pieces together; second, as described by Fromm in his forgotten book *The Forgotten Lan-*

guage (Fromm 1951), one relies primarily on one's intuitive grasp of the meaning as a whole. These two approaches are not necessarily separate, and, indeed, it is sometimes difficult to distinguish between an association and an intuitive grasp of a symbolic meaning. I will give an example of a dream in which both ways of interpreting were relevant.

Rosemary told me the following dream:

"I was in a church. I was emotionally pulled toward the warmth of a woman and her daughter against the influence of a priest who was pale, bald, and cold.

"There was a magpie in a cage. I was sure that if I let the magpie out, the priest would be furious with me. I fiddled with the lock and accidentally let the bird out. I was terrified. The church door was open, and outside it was a beautiful sunny day with blue skies. I tried to shut the door but couldn't. Then I became afraid that the bird would put droppings all over the congregation and that that would also anger the priest.

"The priest then appeared and I admitted to him what had happened, but to my surprise, he did not appear to be angry.

"Earlier in the night I had a shorter dream. I was struggling in sand, and there was a horrible wood louse with fierce eyes. I thought he would bore into me and eat me up."

The priest reminded Rosemary of a man in her local health-food shop, which is organized by a group who favor alternative ways of living and eating. She is ambivalent toward people of this kind; they seem to her to be living in an unreal world of their own, yet she agrees with their basic beliefs and often feels a revulsion against meat, hates preparing it, and thinks of becoming a vegetarian.

Magpies, she went on, steal things. The bird also reminded her that a jackdaw is said to pick up sparkling jewelry.

The church recalled her hatred of its powerful life-deadening influence in her early years and of an interview the day before by a man who "preached" at her in a dominating way, "typical" of men, especially when they are in positions of power. He had the manner of a clergyman, and she felt a revulsion toward him.

The woman in the dream was an actual friend whom she liked and who had recently talked to her about greed.

I took up the matter of greed, and said that I thought that the terrifying wood louse represented her own appetites that she feared might get out of control, to which she replied that recently she had been compulsively and ravenously eating, whereas sometimes she would go to the other extreme and deprive herself of food.

A caged animal is such an apt and widespread symbol of repressed passions that the bird seemed an obvious example of this. Rosemary herself made this interpretation, as well as several others, and there was, by and large, agreement between us as to the various meanings in the dream. The droppings presumably referred to her rage at being caged.

Because she told me the dream toward the end of a session, we had no more time to explore it. And, of course, we may not have gained much further insight had we done so. The conflict it depicted between her appetites and the crushing force of a cold, male-dominated internal world seems clear enough. The dream was a useful confirmation of matters that we had discussed, and it expressed them in a powerful and moving way.

The only interpretation I offered that Rosemary had not made herself was that the church represented psychotherapy. She had at times, I reminded her, complained that I used psychotherapy to promote my own male urges to dominate and seduce women. I did not get around to suggesting that the priest may stand for me; this interpretation seems plausible, as, first, Rosemary is a bit confused as to whether I am "orthodox" or "alternative"; second, the priest's surprisingly benign response may represent my own nonpunitive stance in the face of her rage; and third, she knows that I had a religious upbringing.

THE DISADVANTAGES OF FREUD'S RECOMMENDATIONS

The way in which the therapist orientates his investigation will depend on his theory of psychotherapy. If he believes that people become neurotic primarily because family and society have conveyed a distorted and conflictual view of the world inimical to the development of a coherent and realistic self-image, he will do all in his power to present a clear, unambiguous, and full account of things and will tend to accept and encourage the patient's view of himself. If, however, with Freud, he believes that people become ill primarily because they try to deny their primitive fantasies, he will focus on resistance to the truth and will be suspicious of the patient's account of himself— an attitude that Freud described as "benevolent scepticism." In his search for the hidden fantasies and the way in which they distort present reality, the therapist will need to provide a setting in which they will most easily arise and be seen.

The very fact of listening quietly and without condemnation will (as I suggested in the previous chapter) go a long way toward this goal. But, in his papers on technique (Freud 1958), which continue to command wide respect, Freud advocated a method designed to take us further. A word that he used to describe the essence of this technique was *abstinence*. The analyst must not, on any account, preempt the patient's fantasies by revealing the truth about himself. If asked a question, he does not reply. Not only will fantasies thereby be given free rein, Freud believed, but they will appear in pure form uninfluenced by a knowledge of the therapist's character, way of life, or views on the matter in question. Furthermore, the pressing urges of the patient must not be assuaged by a comforting or gratifying word or action lest its full force be lost. To put it another way, the traumatic experiences of the patient that led to his downfall and that tend to reappear in therapy must be suffered again before they can be fully assimilated. It is a harsh doctrine, and one wonders how much it is the fruit of Freud's stoical and pessimistic attitude to life rather than a balanced approach to the task. Nevertheless, it is a strategy that makes a lot of sense.

In everyday life, it is taken for granted that people are often extremely reluctant to hear unpalatable truths about themselves. And even if they appear to accept such truths, it can be observed that they have means of invalidating or distancing themselves from these insights. Freud's theory of defense and his technique for dealing with resistance is but an elaboration of this aspect of human intercourse. The psychotherapist who underestimates the intensity and persistence of the patient's desperate wish to remain oblivious of certain facts is in for a bad time. Defenses against truth—schizoid, paranoid, obsessional, hysterical, and so on—have been extensively categorized in psychoanalytical literature. What I wish to emphasize at this point is the sheer power of the defensive patient; the variety, subtlety, and individuality of his strategies; and the risk of the therapist being brainwashed when faced with formidable persuasiveness and charm. That the therapist's need to armor himself against this danger should have led to the almost impregnable buttress that constitutes psychoanalytical technique is understandable yet lamentable. Certainly, as I have suggested earlier, the analytic attitude—the stance of a reflective, patient, and tolerant listener—has much to commend it. But a technique that requires the degree of withholding and impersonality that Freud advised is another matter. There would have to be a convincing reason for employing such a restrictive device, and it is debatable whether such a reason can be found.

This question is central to all those whose practice of psychotherapy has been deeply influenced by Freud. It touches upon many aspects of behavior in the consulting room, for example, whether or not it is permissible to touch patients or reassure them, the use of the couch, the degree of formality that is desirable, and so on. I referred to this issue in the previous chapter, and because of its importance I confront the matter from various points of view throughout the book. Although it is clear that fantasies and illusions will not readily manifest themselves if the therapist intrudes with precipitate reactions to, or hasty reassurances about, the patient's words, such reticence need not necessarily depart as far from other kinds of human discourse as does orthodox psychoanalysis. There would appear to be no reason why the therapist should not correct a misperception *after* he has given it a chance to emerge. If the patient were to say, for example, "I think you kept me waiting in order to see whether I got angry," the reasons for her fantasy could be explored before the actuality of what happened be confronted. It might be important for her to know whether she was right or not, and she can only rely on the therapist's honesty and self-knowledge to help her make this assessment.

The question of frustration is a variation of the same

problem. To what extent should the therapist, by word or action, reassure and comfort the patient? If there is blandness and overprotectiveness, the patient's deepest anguish may be kept well away from the light of day, yet most of those who come for therapy have a profound and legitimate need for validation. One can go wrong either way. I am not pretending that such judgments are easy. I am, however, anxious to convey my belief that they should not be influenced by a conviction that reassurance must be avoided like the plague.

The tenet that there can be a rule for all people and all situations stems from a failure to recognize the diversity of human beings. How can we know whether it is important to withhold certain responses to a patient unless we have learned their particular meaning to her? Moreover, the experience of frustration and the negative feelings engendered by this may well increase the patient's reluctance to expose her vulnerability. We reveal ourselves to those we trust and love. The therapist who says, as it were, "I must be cruel to be kind" should be sure of his ground, or he will seem like the parent who insists that the child go to bed for his own sake rather than for the parent's need of peace and quiet.

Most writings on the subject convey that interpretations take place in a disciplined and orderly context. But are they a true account of what takes place in the consulting room? A discrepancy between what practitioners write and what they actually do is inevitably confusing to those who wish to learn about the beliefs of those experienced in the work. When, in my writing, I have criticized the orderly approach, my own critics have taken me to task on two counts: first, that psychotherapists, in their daily work, are much more flexible and spontaneous than I give them credit for, and second, that it is all very well for me at this stage of my career to transcend the "rules of technique," but that the poor student needs to learn and abide by them until he has sufficient confidence to break free. In response to the latter argument, I would say that although guidelines to a student are helpful, it is dangerous to encourage a beginner to practice a method in which one does not really believe oneself.

With these thoughts in mind, I shall give a sketch of a session in which interpretations were made. I have selected it from my work today, and it is as random as I can manage. I do not set it up as a model, for in this work there can be no model to suit the personality of the individual practitioner. But perhaps it will at least show the way in which understanding can occur in a session that is hardly notable for organization or order and is, in fact, rather messy.

Vicky arrived a quarter of an hour late, drenched by a thunderstorm, bringing, as she often does, her 2-year-old daughter.

"I'm sorry I'm late," she said. "I forgot the time. I was in the bath and suddenly remembered."

"Is your hair wet from the rain or the bath?"

"From the bath." Vicky sat down, and the toddler came over to me, showing me seashells and chatting. Vicky also started talking, and I found it all a bit distracting but did not want to reject the little girl, who eventually started playing on the floor and focusing more on her mother.

"You know you say my depression is due to anger," said Vicky. "Well, I think there's more to it than that. I'm wishing my life away. I kill time. I'm always living in the future and not in the present."

I agreed with her that this was so, and she went on to tell me that over the weekend she had stayed at a bed-and-breakfast. During the night, going to the bathroom, she had become terrified of the utter darkness and feared she might fall. After that she couldn't get back to sleep and thought of death.

Vicky, whose father was killed when she was a child, often thinks of death and is terrified that I may die. We had been over this theme many times, and I saw little point in referring to it again. Moreover, she continued with the previous theme.

"Death makes me think of killing time. I'm not living properly. I always want to be doing something else."

"What's wrong with just being in the here-and-now?"

"I don't know. I just feel dislocated."

"And distant?"

"Yes. There's a film between me and the world. Sometimes it feels like a slight headache. I'm self-conscious. You remember my telling you I can't go through a door without wondering whether people think I'm doing it O.K.?"

"Yes. I think you're living in your image, not in yourself. I think you feel you *are* what people think you are."

"Why do I do this?"

"You tried very hard to match up to your parents' image of you, didn't you? Do you think they were disappointed in you?"

"Well, it was more that they didn't *see* me. They thought I was happy, and I appeared to be happy, and they were satisfied with that. But I had to live up to this."

"So that's what you still try to do: to be what people think you are. This makes me think of my chronic complaint that you nearly always qualify my interpretations. You say, 'Yes, but it's not *quite* like that.' And often the qualification doesn't seem to me to make all that difference. You crave to be understood, don't you, and doubt if it's possible?"

"Yes, I do."

During this conversation, Vicky became more and more animated and leaned forward in her chair. She didn't seem at all distant—indeed, she felt very real and close. I did not notice this at the time, probably because I myself felt close to her.

At the end of the session, Vicky changed the theme and asked me a question about myself. I answered honestly, which meant revealing that I had a problem at the moment. On questioning, I told her something about it. She looked concerned and sympathetic, offered some useful comments, and suggested a practical matter in which she might, in a small way, be helpful. I thanked her and accepted her offer.

I do not think that I showed particular acumen in this session, and another therapist may well have spotted valuable connections that I missed. But I believe that it was, to use Winnicott's simple but very helpful phrase, "good enough."

It is often said that beginners interpret too frequently, that in their enthusiasm for a newfound technique and before they have reached the age of wisdom, they are premature in voicing the connections they see between the patient's words and their knowledge of theory. This is no doubt true, but there is more to it than that.

We are all, I believe, enthralled with the wonders of interpretation. Even a century after the birth of psychoanalysis, it is fascinating and satisfying to watch the emergence of oedipal conflicts, sibling rivalries, and, especially, transference fantasies in the patient's words and actions. We have an ever-ready tool at our disposal to help us when we are lost. But herein lies its danger. Because it is so useful, because it gives us a focus, a meaning, and a possible action when we are lost, the temptation to rely on it too heavily and to orientate our whole relationship with the patient around it is great. What are the disadvantages of so doing?

First, we may impose on the patient a meaning that depends more on our theories and our own experience than on the reality of his life, a blatant and momentous example of which is Freud's unflattering and narrow-minded conception of women. To impose an inappropriate meaning is particularly damaging if, as is not infrequently the case, one aspect of the patient's problem is that her early perception of herself has been invalidated by those around her. And second, a focus on interpretation, with a map in hand for guidance, restricts the relationship to a unidimensional one. The therapist watches the patient, who, in turn, is aware of being watched. This process is bound to have a major effect on the quality of the encounter. We see the patient in very special circumstances and learn little of how she might respond in a more mutual and ordinary situation. Moreover, the patient is placed in a passive situation, unable to make her own contribution to understanding what is happening.

Hitherto in this chapter I have considered interpretation, in keeping with common psychoanalytic usage, as a verbal communication aimed at casting new light on the patient's words or actions. However, as I have discussed elsewhere (Lomas 1987), the therapist's whole response is itself a form of interpretation. We cannot have a dialogue with another human being without revealing our views of life. Every gesture and every response make a comment on the way we see the world and the way we see the other person; and, although there may be no explicit comment or criticism, we implicitly convey a value judgment. If my patient's sick humor makes me laugh, it validates her own belief, which might be tentative, that this kind of humor is not really sick and that humor has a part in the most serious of undertakings. On the other hand, if I do not laugh at a patient's tedious and repetitive joke-telling, I convey my belief that there is something wrong with such activity and may provoke her to question it herself.

It is sometimes said that a good therapist sets an example to his patient, a model that can be internalized, for example, as a child may learn how to live by observing his parents. This idea gives me some uneasiness. Are we therapists so perfect that we can take on such a responsibility? However, without laying claim to this superiority, we can, I believe, act in such a way with the patient that we will show her where she is failing. We can, for example, keep our nerve when she is falling apart, implying that she is seeing the situation in a distorted way. The set-up of the consulting room enables us to present our view of the world and our attitude to the patient in a relatively balanced way, to be, in a sense, at our most mature. This stance has, of course, its dangers, which I discuss in more detail later, and it is a poor model for a patient whose defense against the hazards of living is a perpetual state of calmness. Nevertheless, the therapist who can, by experience, nature, and the good fortune of liking his patient, maintain a calm attitude while not excluding the passion of committed living will be likely to bring insights to her in ways that would not usually be regarded as making interpretations.

Although I have contrasted ways of relating that are different from that of formal interpretation, I do not wish to convey a dichotomy, for the manner in which a verbal interpretation is made is suffused with the therapist's whole personality. This point has been emphasized by Joseph Natterson (1991), who asserts that the psychotherapist's focus on the formal aspect of the interpretation is too narrow. He writes:

> In many instances, this narrowness may coexist with a favour-
> able result, although the basic mutative factors may be miscon-

strued or overlooked. Alternatively, the therapist utters the "correct" ideas but conveys inappropriate and negating nonverbal messages by tone of voice, choice of words, facial expression, posture, gestures, and related signals. The patient's reactions are to the latter communications (the subtext), but the therapist may defensively continue to attend only to the verbal "correctness" of the interpretation. Circumstances like these indicate why interpretation should be defined as the total communication and why the nonexplicit components of interpretation should be known to the interpreter. [p. 58]

Natterson believes (and it is a rare belief among psychotherapists) that the choice of manner in which the practitioner makes a particular interpretation should not be relegated to the bland phrase "the art of therapy" but be subject to the rigorous thinking we bestow on the verbal interpretation itself.

In recent years, under the influence of contemporary philosophy and linguistics, the idea has arisen, and taken root, that it doesn't really matter whether an interpretation is true or not. This view has been cogently expressed by Donald Spence (1982), who believes that the pursuit of historical truth should be replaced by an acceptance that narrative truth is all we can hope for—and is, indeed, enough for our purposes. As long as we enable the patient to go away with a more coherent picture of his life, we have done our job. In the "Sherlock Holmes Tradition," as Spence puts it (1987), case reports are always presented as if the interpretation proposed is the only interpretation possible. The therapist indulges in a "narrative smoothing," imposing his own meaning on the patient's account, a meaning that satisfies him intellectually, morally, and aesthetically and that he then tries to get the patient to accept. If done well, he provides a satisfying coherence instead of fragmentation and discontinuity.

That this occurs is certainly the case. Our problem is to decide whether we are content with it. The question we are faced with is the extent to which it is necessary—and indeed inevitable—that in the course of healing, we need to create illusion in our patients. We may acknowledge that fictions are necessary to make life bearable, but the healing power of truth must also be taken into consideration. An overwhelming factor in the development of illness is the confusion that occurs when people avoid the truth or are prevented by others from reaching it. In view of this, it would seem that we should make our interpretations as close to reality as is possible for us.

Chapter Six

The Use and Abuse of Transference

Occasionally one gets the impression that a part of what we call the transference situation is actually not a spontaneous manifestation of feelings in the patient, but is created by the analytically produced situation, that is, artificially created by the analytic technique.

—Sandor Ferenczi

The term *transference* is used to denote the process by which a patient displaces onto his therapist attitudes that he had adopted toward previous figures in his life. His feelings, thoughts, and responses are inappropriate in the present situation; it is as though he were stuck in the past.

The phenomenon of transference is not confined to the consulting room. We all, at times, relate to others as though they were the people who had once made a powerful impact on us. It cannot be otherwise. The lessons we learn in early life will not be discarded every time we meet a new person or situation, for they are a useful guide to what we might expect in the future. But they are not always as useful as might be hoped. In particular, if such lessons have been engraved on our personalities with undue force, they will be too rigid to accommodate to the varieties of experience we encounter in later life.

In psychotherapy, the transference emerges more starkly than elsewhere because the patient is in the presence of someone who seems able to provide more richness than any other person in life since childhood, except possibly an adored lover. The hope of understanding and help provides an intense yearning for intimacy and a terror of rejection. When hope is uppermost, the therapist is likely to be idealized as a savior, but if she appears to fail, she may be seen as a tormentor and become the target of hate. But quite apart from these passionate extremes, the patient will reveal ideas and feelings derived from all the memories and fantasies that he has accumulated during his life. By comparing these inappropriate attitudes with the reality of the present relationship, the therapist can gain an immensely valuable understanding of the patient's dilemma. If, for example, the patient has a firm belief, without any evidence to support it, that the therapist has elaborate plans to marry him, we know that something odd is going on, and we can rest comfortably on our theory.

I shall not, at this point, give an example of transference, for it is such a ubiquitous phenomenon that most of the vignettes that I present in this book bear witness to the way, in dreams and fantasies, one can so often see that the drama often includes veiled references to the therapist. For example, in the dream reported in the previous chapter, the priest and the church would seem to refer to the moralistic attitude that the patient consistently attributed to me but that had much to do with her constricting and puritanical upbringing.

When the past is evoked with a degree of emotional intensity that is well-nigh intolerable to the patient, we refer to the reemergence of a trauma. In order for this to occur, the circumstances of the therapy must be sufficiently near to the original trauma to strike a chord. The mere fact of placing oneself in another's hands in a situation that is inevitably frustrating and uncertain may be enough provocation. What is important is that the therapeutic set-up should be both sufficiently close to, yet sufficiently different from, the original experience to ensure that the patient does not remain encased in his anguish and can see a way to a better outcome.

Despite the tremendous gain that the concept of transference brings to the therapist's capacity to understand, there are certain pitfalls to be considered. When two people meet, the truth lies between them. Neither of them has a privileged access to it. If a disagreement develops, there is a temptation to invalidate the other's point of view, adducing whatever reasons one can find for believing he is in error. We know from our experience of daily life and the political and intellectual scene that unhappily this is the case. The technique of transference interpretation, however, is largely based on the theory that only *one* of the parties wishes to invalidate the other. The patient, it is thought, is desperate to maintain his tenuous hold on comforting illusions and will go to any lengths to contradict the insights of the therapist. The latter, by contrast, is assumed to have only the patient's interests at heart and to approach the task with the detached objectivity of the scientist, a belief that is itself a comforting illusion. I am not suggesting that in practice psychotherapists inevitably polarize the situation in this way, but that the theory encourages them to do so. What is omitted in this view of the matter is the patient's own search for the truth and the therapist's wish to retain her professional esteem and maintain her own vision of the world.

COUNTERTRANSFERENCE

The psychoanalytic frame of reference does, however, include a concept designed to mitigate the practitioner's bias, namely countertransference. To what extent is it successful in doing so?

Freud originally used the term *countertransference* to describe the analyst's transference onto the patient, that is to say, the distortion of her perception of the patient because of her own rigid assumptions from the past. In order to minimize the countertransference, Freud advocated that the practitioner place herself in the hands of a psychoanalyst in order to have

thology; it may be a desperate plea for a needed response by the therapist or even a criticism of the way the latter is failing (Langs 1978; see also Casement 1985).

There is a paradox in that we need to recognize that transference and countertransference are part of the therapeutic process but do not constitute it, yet to separate these phenomena from the total experience is, except perhaps in theory, beyond our capacity. We live with the patient; we participate fully in the drama of therapy; we cannot be sure much of the time whether the behavior of either of us is pathological or healthy; and we often cannot discern whether our attitudes emanate from ourselves or are reactions to each other. Moreover, an overscrupulous attention to these conceptions may inhibit a spontaneous response, which might be of more importance to the patient than anything else that the therapist could do or say. Such a response has a ring of authenticity and may be the only kind of communication that the patient will bother to take seriously—particularly if he is profoundly wary of any hint of control or manipulation.

An unsettled debate among therapists focuses on whether the practitioner should merely use his "countertransference" as a guide or whether he should openly confess it to the patient. If one accepts the psychoanalytically orthodox view that the therapist should not disclose his feelings, there is no decision to make. However, if one is not restricted by this rule, it can be seen that there are certain advantages in disclosure. First, it is a direct and powerful way of bringing the patient's attention, in a situation where this may be bearable, to the effect he has on others. Second, it puts the phenomenon into an area of mutuality. If the therapist were to say, for example, "My mind keeps wandering during this session, and I don't know why. I don't think it's me. As far as I know I'm not tired or distracted. Is it something you are doing to me? Perhaps you're not talking about what is really important to you?" Then the matter can be discussed and the patient can make a contribution of his own. And the assertion is being made in a way that is likely to be more acceptable than "God, you're boring." However, though tact and delicacy have their place in therapy, they can be carried too far and be seen as merely a hypocritical and stereotyped formula of politeness, for example, the politician who is about to say something really nasty begins, "With the greatest respect . . ." As in so many areas in psychotherapy, much depends on getting to know the patient. There are people to whom one might quite easily say, "You're a bloody fool," and others who would be annihilated by such a comment.

As with the interpretation of transference, so with the disclosure of "countertransference," timing is crucial. If we are to put ourselves in a good position to receive the impact of the patient on the less conscious part of ourselves, we must allow some time—if only a moment—in which to have a naive experience of him. In other words, we must be prepared to play our role (say, that of overprotective parent), which needs to be understood, before we collect ourselves together and reveal to him his effect upon us. (An example of the long period of time in which therapists may sometimes need to expose their vulnerability to the power of the patient's transference before becoming fully aware of it and able to communicate it effectively is given in Chapter 10.)

THE DANGERS OF INTENSE TRANSFERENCE

Because transference is a universal phenomenon, the patient is likely to be deeply enmeshed in a tumultuous relationship with others in his daily life—his spouse, his lover, his children, his boss, and so forth—and he may also develop disturbingly passionate feelings toward them while in therapy. The transferences that are already in situ are often useful indications of the patient's psyche. But strong transferences to others that may appear during the course of therapy may well constitute a defensive displacement of unacceptable feelings toward the therapist and result in the type of behavior outside the consulting room that psychoanalysts refer to as *acting out*. On the other hand, narcissistic feelings in the therapist can easily lead him to mistakenly attribute a developing new relationship in the patient's life to a mere disguise for the latter's love toward him and overlook the possibility that if the patient embarks on a love relationship while in therapy, this may be the consequence of an increased capacity for love that has been awakened by the treatment, in which case the move is a creative rather than a defensive one. Moreover, there are dangers in *not* acting out. The intensity of the patient's undiluted transference love for his therapist may be such that his ordinary relationships are impoverished or mutilated. One has to balance this potential error against the necessity to assess as accurately as possible the real behavior of those around the patient. In such a situation, we are dependent, as in so many areas of psychotherapy, on a careful assessment of the individual case, without jumping to conclusions based on a generalized theory or our own blind spots. For example, we may easily neglect the current impact of the family network upon the patient and may even find ourselves treating someone who is primarily a victim of forces better confronted by a family therapist.

The early psychoanalysts declined to accept patients who were about to embark on an important relationship such as marriage. This is now considered to be unjustifiably rigid and is no longer current practice. Nevertheless, they had a point. The intensity of the transference can be formidably intrusive to those in ordinary life, and we should perhaps keep in mind the

question, "Can transference wreck a marriage?" before we encourage it to flower. As I have suggested earlier, transference will
appear whatever one does. What is important is to recognize it
and be as aware as possible of its likely effects. Like any other
experience, it can be stifled if badly received or, if given undue
significance, raised to an artificial level in which it becomes
addictive and destructive.

Chapter Seven

Formulations of Anguish

There's a cool web of language winds us in,
Retreat from too much joy or too much fear:
We grow sea-green at last and coldly die
In brininess and volubility.

—Robert Graves

States of human anguish and incapacity have been formulated in different ways throughout the ages. Sometimes people describe their condition in terms that are unusual in our culture. A young woman, the subject of Marion Milner's book *The Hands of the Living God* (1969), came to the author saying that she had "lost her soul." I doubt if her predicament could have been put in a better way.

Because everyone is unique, there is no possibility of producing a formula that will adequately describe a particular person or the problem that he brings to the therapist. This does not mean, however, that we must eschew concepts altogether, for to do so would be to abolish language. Words are approximations to our experience of living, and we have to use them despite their limitations. Language, as Wittgenstein has argued, is a function of usage, and, to an extent, psychotherapists have created their own language from the pressure of their peculiar work. Unhappily, under the influence of a mistaken quest for the relative certainty of natural science and a desire to sound authoritative, therapists have also created a confused and bewildering variety of unnecessary terms, many of which bear only a tenuous connection with the actual practice of psychotherapy. This is most notable in the case of attempts to conceptualize what is wrong with those people who present themselves for treatment. As a first approach to the subject, I shall consider the negative features that are most often apparent in those who seek help, while recognizing that any list is bound to be arbitrary, and that I do injustice to qualities of courage and hope and to the richness and complexity of living. In brief, patients are defensive, insecure, ashamed, and confused. I will take these attitudes in order.

The fact that people are defensive, that unwittingly they endeavor to thwart the therapist's attempts to unravel the truth, was one of Freud's major findings. I will return to this phenomenon later, simply noting at this point that various forms of defense frequently dominate the picture. This has a particular relevance to what follows because it is often only when defensiveness has been eroded that the deepest fears and griefs become apparent.

Second, insecurity manifests itself nakedly as anxiety or terror. Freud originally believed that the child experienced a trauma too overwhelming to be assimilated, the result of which was twofold. The child attempted thereafter to avoid all such situations or, indeed, anything that reminded him of the situation; however, from time to time, he recreated the trauma in attempts to master it. The trauma theory gradually lost ground in favor of the idea that the child's fear derived from the fantasied consequences of his desires, although the writings of the Hungarian psychoanalyst Sandor Ferenczi were an important exception to this trend. In more recent years, however, the theory has emerged in a new guise. This view has been most poignantly expressed by Winnicott, who describes the child's terror when let down by his environment. It is, he maintains, the psychological equivalent of being physically dropped by his mother. (The appropriate response, when this kind of experience is relived by the adult patient, is a matter that I discuss in the next chapter.)

Third, those who feel shame describe their agony in many ways. They are unworthy, unlovable, incapable, empty, evil, guilty, sick, mad, a nuisance to everyone, different from others, do not belong to the human race, are unfit to live, and so on. Something has happened that, it seems, has convinced them that they are unlovable. Indeed, it may have been that, in childhood, for whatever reason, they were unloved, or loved in the wrong way, or that they were misfits. Once they have lost hope, many things then follow that worsen the situation. Fury, derived from anguish, will add to their feeling of guilt, and the failure of autonomous and creative development will endorse the feeling of inadequacy.

Fourth, confusion is always present, and sometimes central, in emotional distress. In Chapter 9, I discuss the sources of confusion that are external to the child and beyond his capacity to unravel. But confusion will also arise from his own attempts to evade reality by denying the existence of unacceptable aspects of his experience or constructing an alternative reality of bewitching plausibility as a substitute for hatred, despair, and a sense of futility. And, finally, confusion may be manufactured to act as a smoke screen and undermine the attempts of others to gain understanding of the problem.

FREUD'S THEORY OF PSYCHOPATHOLOGY

Let us now take a further look at the most comprehensive theory of psychopathology that has yet emerged—that of psychoanalysis. Freud showed us that symptoms have meaning, thereby opening a whole new way of understanding, charting, and

classifying the various forms of psychological disturbance that
afflict us and, indeed, making considerable progress himself in
mapping this territory. He saw psychopathology as a consequence of conflict between aim and that which made the aim
appear frightening—in his terms, between instinctual drive and
defense mechanisms. His explanatory achievement is so creative
that the efforts of psychoanalysis to enlarge it sometimes appear
as little more than footnotes to his work. Although Freud was
no armchair theoretician (indeed, his dedication to understand
what actually occurred in the consulting room is remarkable),
the theory he evolved was influenced by preconceptions derived
from the physical sciences that had little to do with actual
people. It is surprising, and a measure of his genius, that with
such an inappropriate basis for his theories he taught us so
much.

The present-day theory of psychopathology is a mess. This
is, to an extent, the inevitable consequence of a mistaken
attempt to formulate a *comprehensive* theory; but the situation
has been made worse by the fact that psychoanalysts who have
been original and brave enough to remedy Freud's mistakes have
either departed from the fold and constructed their own theories
or tried too hard to preserve, as far as possible, the sanctity of the
word. Although there is no substitute for reading the original
work, a heroic account of the literature of Freud and his
followers was made in 1935 by Fenichel (1946). No one, as far as
I know, has since attempted a comparable feat. At this point I
will do no more than briefly outline the basic conception.

Freud believed that his greatest achievement was to chart
the ways in which our unacceptable experience (the repressed
unconscious) manifests itself in dreams, fantasies, symptoms,
and inappropriate behavior and has a logic quite distinct from
that of our conscious thought. For example, one image may
represent several ideas and memories. Freud's emphasis was on

the repression of desire, and his theory of psychopathology is based on the vicissitudes that the sexual and aggressive instincts (the id) undergo in the face of the ego's attempt to ward off anxiety. Various defense mechanisms—splitting, projection, and so forth—are brought to bear on the primitive drives in order to make them manageable. This theory gave psychotherapists a guideline with which to explore the unconscious and helped them to tap their own intuitive understanding of the symbolism of dreams and symptoms. The value of the approach can hardly be overstated. Yet it is essentially a dehumanizing theory. The nature of the conflict is expressed in terms of forces and resistances as though we were dealing with a problem of thermodynamics. The infant is thought to be more concerned with the discharge of energy than with reaching out to a meaningful world. Indeed, Freud was less impressed with the child's attraction to what is around him than with the narcissistic wish to remain in a homeostatic, hermetically sealed, womb-like state. Moreover, he was not very interested in the unique circumstances that a particular child was forced to meet, being more concerned with universals: the hurdles and disappointments (such as weaning, separation, rivalry) with which we all are faced. This direction of his thinking has been taken further by many of his followers, notably Melanie Klein, who laid great emphasis on the infant's tendency to split his perceptual world. Thus, the conception of psychopathology that dominates psychoanalytic thought today is that of fragmentation. Whether the self is conceived as fragmented from the start, as Freud and Melanie Klein believe, or begins as a whole that is later undermined by frustrating experiences, as Fairbairn maintains, pathology is described in terms of parts of the self at war with each other. There are two serious disadvantages of this way of thinking.

First, because it is schematic and oversimplified, it can

easily lead us into a state of arrogant certainty. The authorial voice in accounts of our work becomes (to use the language of the literary critics) declamatory rather than interrogative. The patient moves from the schizoid-paranoid to the depressive position, or in Lacan's terms from the *Imaginary* to the *Real* world, or is fixated at the anal stage of development, and so on. Much that is written about ideas that stir the imagination and find a form of words for elusive states of minds is often illuminating. If, however, we take it as an authoritative account of reality, then we lose sight of the patient, fail to recognize the endless depths of the human mind, and no longer look to him to surprise us with his own spontaneity and sudden insights. And second, the patient is conceived as a passive thing at the mercy of mechanical forces, without will, without moral purpose, without choice, and without responsibility. He does not choose whether to become well or ill or what form the illness shall take.

The most powerful critique of the mechanistic character of psychoanalytic theory has been made by the existential analysts (Binswanger 1963, Boss 1963), who, with intellectual rigor, argue the case for the uniqueness and agency of human beings, the importance of choice and responsibility, and the fact that we live in a moral world, and who write with moving eloquence of the significance of death and the "inauthentic" way of living of those of us who seek distraction rather than face our mortality. The seminal writings of the theologians Buber (1961) and Tillich (1952) are convincing and inspiring and take us into another universe. Paradoxically, for a movement that should by its own tenets lead us down from esoteric intellectual heights and place us fair-square in the marketplace, no body of work in the field has accumulated more tormented and obscure philosophical reasoning than that of those existential therapists who have turned to the thinking of Heidegger, Kierkegaard, and Sartre. Moreover, this school of thought has made, perhaps on principle, little attempt to describe the particular defenses and confusions that we meet daily in the consulting room. Let me hastily add that in saying this I do not mean to dismiss their work, which I regard as among the most valuable available to us, nor necessarily to reject the ideas of the philosophers themselves. What I believe has happened is that this particular group of thinkers have been overwhelmed by professional philosophy rather than stimulated thereby to enhance and formulate their ordinary, day-to-day experience of therapy.

Where does psychoanalysis stand on this matter today? The situation is intriguing, provocative, and frustrating. For several decades, there has been an increasing dissatisfaction among analysts with the limitations of Freudian theory. Winnicott, in particular, has done much to promote recognition of the importance of spontaneity. He persuasively stresses the child's search for meaning and, when writing about patients, conveys his belief that they are in some control of their destiny. Shafer, Kohut, Bion, and, most notably, several members of the "Independent" group of British psychoanalysts explore, in their various ways, a belief in the centrality of empathy, the significance of Keats's concept of negative capability, the essential wholeness of the person, the human relationship in the therapeutic encounter, and so forth, thereby indicating an urge to move away from established theory. Yet the need for a radical new perspective is not seen. We await the new Freud and in the meantime must make as best use as we can of the rich, albeit piecemeal, insights that have been passed down to us.

In order to counteract mechanistic and reductive theories, it is not necessary to endorse some of the extravagances of the romantic and humanistic idealization of man's freedom. The recent critique of these movements by the deconstructionists has some justification but unhappily leads us in the direction of nihilism. In our daily lives, we do believe that the self exists, and that we have some measure of freedom, individuality, and responsibility; and it should be the same with our work. In our attempt to understand people, we should bring to bear everything that we have experienced in our lives from our contact with loved and unloved ones, the insights into existence that we gain from the creations of the wise and gifted, and the gut feeling that is a distillation of all that we know and which, for want of a better word, we call intuition. And we should try to avoid the danger of failing to accept tragedy in the lives of our patients by formulae that play it down. Recognizing, therefore, the severe limitations of the theory of psychopathology, let us try to assess its relevance in the consulting room. The question for the practicing psychotherapist is, "In what way is the theory useful to me in practice?"

The best answer that I can give is that the various descriptions that have been made of defense mechanisms present a kind of crude map that can guide our thoughts quite quickly into well-known patterns of behavior and can give us a shorthand in order to communicate with colleagues. I have in mind such concepts as denial, splitting, idealization, and projection. Moreover, the descriptions that are given usually contain ideas about what is being defended against. It is not my purpose here to give a detailed account of these formulations, for psychotherapeutic literature is teeming with them either in their original construction by seminal thinkers from Freud onward or in the later condensed accounts of them that are available. And those who wish for simple and authoritative definitions can turn to Rycroft's *Critical Dictionary of Psychoanalysis* (1972).

My own view is that what is most useful in day-to-day work is to have available in one's mind the characteristic fantasies that accompany these psychological maneuvers and to describe them in language that is near to that of daily use and retains, as far as possible, a sense that there is a self behind them (even the psychotic, however impoverished, retains some of this sense). The more we move toward abstract formulations, the greater the danger that our imaginative powers will be curbed, and that we will be confined to well-trodden and narrow paths. Although developmental theory can contribute to the understanding of adult psychopathology, it is, in its present state of uncertainty, less useful than might be expected.

CONFUSIONS OF DIAGNOSIS

It is in the area of diagnosis that confused thinking is most apparent. The tradition of converting patients into clinical entities has been passed down from the doctor and the psychiatrist, and despite the fact that psychotherapists are less likely to regard their patient's pain as a manifestation of physical disorder, the habit of labeling remains.

Although it is useful to find words to describe certain destructive or impoverished ways of behaving which the psychotherapist comes to recognize with sufficient frequency to identify and wish to study, the disadvantage is that when people are categorized, the human being is easily lost. In the case of psychopathological diagnoses, there is a further complication. Freud helped us *despite* a theory of child development that was immensely flawed. The same is true of Melanie Klein. And Winnicott found insight through an inspired intuition (recalling the early theory of trauma) that bypassed both Freud and Klein while renouncing neither of them. Outside the consulting room we gain most, I believe, by being with children and remembering our own childhood.

In health we are, more or less, a coherent whole. The sicker we are, the greater our fragmentation. But there is no simple correlation between our apparent capacity to function in society and our lack of real coherence, for fragmentation can be concealed by a superficial adaptation to the world around us. To put it another way, we cannot judge the degree of sickness in a person merely by the severity of his overt symptomatology. Those who work with families are well aware of this problem. A family member who is phobic is not necessarily a more disturbed being than one who maintains a superbly balanced calm. The various forms of fragmentation (denial, projection, displacement, contradiction, and the like) remain, however, an important area of the therapist's understanding. Psychotherapeutic literature bursts at the seams with descriptions and conceptions of these mental gymnastics. Unhappily, because so much of it is confused and confusing, students are advised to seek out those writings that are written with a care for lucidity and a respect for language.

Whatever we may think about the drawbacks of classifying mental states, we have to come to terms with this practice. Terms such as *hysteria* and *paranoia* are in widespread use among both professionals and the general public. We need to demystify these terms as far as possible and harness them to aid our descriptions of psychological states rather than allow them to dominate and cloud our thinking. To do so is a task beyond my own powers. In what follows, I shall only make a few observations and suggestions.

The term *obsessional* calls to mind someone who controls himself and his surroundings with undue care, whose spontaneity is curtailed by meticulous and pedantic attention to detail, who appears to function more like an automaton than a passionate being and is prone to rationalize his behavior. The psychotherapist may have views about the origin of this sort of attitude to life, that, for example, it is based on a fear of disintegration or a need to repress violent feelings, but it does not follow that she is entitled to regard it as a clinical entity for which a distinct therapeutic approach is indicated. If there is no clinical entity, there is no clear-cut method of treating such a state of mind; but if, as suggested above, we focus on the patient's defensive *measures*, we can suggest ways of relating that may be useful. For example, most therapists would, I imagine, believe that it is usually a waste of time to get locked into argument with someone who defends his position obsessionally. Indeed, the intellectual defense of some well-educated patients constitutes a formidable hurdle for the majority of psychotherapists who have themselves an intellectual background and are easy prey to the seductive charms of logic and learning.

When we come to consider the hysterical frame of mind, we are in a more complex world, and one that has proved much more difficult to formulate. The theory of hysteria is utterly confused. Rycroft (1972) observes that Freud never wrote a definitive formulation of his views on hysteria, and it is, in fact, extremely difficult to discover what is the classical theory of hysteria. The repression of conflict and its displacement onto bodily symptoms or some external object is regarded as central, but this idea falls far short of explaining the concept. Although sexuality clearly plays a major part, the psychoanalytic view that it originates in the "phallic" stage of childhood makes sense only if one accepts Freud's rather weird notions about female sexual development. In view of this confusion, it may be useful to try to make sense of the term by starting from a simple description.

Hysterical behavior is characterized by excessive excitement, exaggeration, and dramatization. The patient seems positively addicted to crises and makes extravagant claims for the importance of certain feelings or experiences. If we manage to avoid being carried away by his force, intensity, and passion, we will also be able to perceive an attempt to overpower our judgment. The element of performance suggests that the hysterical person depends, for his identity, on the attention of the other, whom he aims to control. It is the attempt by someone who feels weak to get help, affirmation, and love, and it exploits an unfavorable position in order to obtain sympathy. Thus, it is a technique to which women—presumably on account of their socially disadvantaged position—resort more commonly than men. This exploitation of weakness can have dire consequences. The patient in therapy becomes progressively more dependent on someone who is idealized yet feared, and this masochistic frame of mind may easily change over into a paranoid one.

Despite their obvious differences, the hysterical and obsessional stances have much in common. They are both attempts to manipulate: one by persuasive argument, the other by creating an atmosphere that moves people to feel compassion, alarm, and love. And both are ways of controlling anxiety. Obsessionality is an obvious way of doing this; if the world is carefully ordered, it is safe. But the hysterical attempt is more complicated and paradoxical; by exaggerating anxiety, the patient seeks to convince the powerful of the urgency of his case and his need to be looked after.

We are left with the question as to why one of the features of hysteria is said to be a tendency to displace conflict symbolically onto another area of experience, for example, to fear the dentist's drill because it represents a sadistic sexual penetration. This mechanism is not as exclusively a hysterical one as psychoanalytic theory suggests, but it would seem likely that someone who is oriented toward the emotional and nondiscursive mode of being, rather than the cognitive, would be inclined to make such imaginative leaps.

Although there is not, and cannot be, a precise formula for treating a hysterical attitude, there are, as in the case of obsessionality, certain warnings that can be given. The intensity of the patient's emotional plea is sometimes quite overwhelming, especially as one knows that the suffering is genuine even if the case that is being made is unjustified. The dangers to therapist and patient of seductive power is a subject that I confront again in a later chapter.

Since the time of Freud, there has been a shift of interest from hysterical and obsessional neuroses characterized by well-defined symptoms to the more diffuse states known as *character disorders*, in which the pathology is less obvious. The disability that has received most attention and which, in varying degrees of severity, is endemic in our society, is that known as *schizoid*. The schizoid person withdraws from people into a narcissistic world, thus removing himself from the humiliation, pain, dependence, and responsibility that come with love and intimacy. Putting the matter in everyday terms, such a person has, as a result of anger and despair, retreated into a sulk.

Richard is a person who manages his daily life adequately and is very successful in his work, but he lacks a sense of purpose. He reclines in his chair in a position of extreme relaxation and comfort, and I myself, for most of the time, feel at ease in the company of this intelligent and pleasant man. He has what I think of as an aesthetic attitude toward living. He is interested and sometimes even moved by life, but it remains a phenomenon in which he is not quite involved. When I commented that he never criticized me and asked him what came into his mind as a criticism, he said, "Your shoes. I don't like your shoes." But he could get no further than that.

As a consequence of his persistent detachment, I not infrequently find myself asking such questions as, "Why are you coming to me? What do you want of life? What sort of person do you want to be?"

On one occasion he replied to such a question, "I want to be thought nice."

"Is that all?" I said. "Would that do as an epitaph on your grave: 'He was nice'?"

"Yes. I just want to be left alone in peace."

"Don't you want any of the excitement of life?" I asked.

"No," he replied. "I'd do without excitement just to avoid any unpleasantness and be safe."

He then recalled a game he played on the sofa as a child. He was in a sort of sledge, cozy and warm, and outside it was cold and dark and frightening. But he was safe there forever.

Richard had been coming to me a long time.

"Are you getting better?" I asked.

"A little," he replied.

It was, I feel, a reply designed to keep me quiet. I also wondered whether, in view of my countertransference feeling of exasperation at his reply, he was sadistically goading me, the only way he had of showing his hidden fury at the world. But if so, it was far from his consciousness.

I do not know of any shock method that can be usefully applied to the dilemma of treating someone who has withdrawn from the world in despair and made a bearable adjustment to it on the surface, and I find myself waiting for quite long periods of time until a fruitful moment comes when I can make a challenge. In other words, I accept his condition, yet I want to encourage him to go beyond it.

Writing within the framework of psychoanalytic theory, Klein (1932), Fairbairn (1952), Guntrip (1968), and others have greatly illuminated our understanding of schizoid states, but in order to fully convey their sense of the anguish and futility of these states of mind and to elaborate on them, Winnicott (1958) and Laing (1960) have had to resort to more ordinary language.

In the words of Winnicott (1987), for example: "The true self is hidden right away and only emerges under very special conditions if at all. In this defence the patient turns himself into a mental hospital and the true self is a patient hidden away in the back somewhere in a padded cell" (p. 81).

Once again there is a danger of regarding a generally accepted syndrome as though it were a distinct entity and of forgetting the diffuseness and overlap. All psychopathology is a corruption of the self and involves falsity. The obsessional creates a false self based on an almost mechanical control, and the hysteric aims for a self that is charismatically charged. There is, I believe, a particular danger for the therapist who has been illuminated by Winnicott's valuable ideas on a true self waiting for a facilitating environment yet who sees this as a pure entity. The distinction between the person who needs to go back to a primitive state before any real progress can be made and the one who masochistically manipulates himself into a weak and helpless position in the manner that is usually described as hysterical can be (as I suggest in Chapter 8) an extraordinarily difficult one to make. Moreover, the two aims may exist in the same person, and, even more confusingly, a sophisticated patient may use any knowledge he possesses of the work of Winnicott and others in an attempt to convince the therapist of infantile needs that must be met.

My brief account of these widely accepted formulations of disturbed states of mind is, of course, an oversimplification. This is inevitable in a book that does not focus on psychopathology. There is, however, more to it than this, for, even if I had the tongues of angels and unlimited time and space, I could not present to the reader a coherent account of the current theory of psychopathology, for none exists. There is a richness of detail to be found in the psychoanalytic literature that can bring insights to us as we work with clients, but if we read it in the hope of finding a satisfying theory of the varieties of disability with which we are daily faced, we will look in vain. Moreover, any specific theory of human nature, however detailed and complicated, starts from a premise that is itself an oversimplification and is therefore likely to give a distorted picture of the whole. Let me describe, as an example, the paranoid attitude.

A person who is said to be paranoid has an exaggerated belief in the likelihood that others are seeking to harm him, and he usually responds to this perceived threat with hostility. According to psychoanalytic theory, this state of mind is attributable to the mechanism of projection, either, as Freud originally believed, projections of homosexual wishes that then appear as threats, or, as Melanie Klein in particular has stressed, the projection of infantile destructiveness. Although few of us would, I imagine, doubt the paramount importance of projection in this context, the question needs to be asked: "Is this all there is to it? Can there be other reasons for an undue fear of the other's intentions?"

There are, to my mind, serious limitations to the concept. First, it does not take account of the simple fact that if we have experienced harmful behavior toward us or been the subject of hostile fantasy in the past, we shall be on the alert for unwelcome repetitions. Second, in a situation that calls to mind Winnicott's idea that the fear of breakdown is a fear of a breakdown that has already occurred, so, I believe, a paranoid fear of utter disaster at the hands of others may often refer back to the traumatic experience of an overwhelming defeat that has been denied and contradicted. Third, it omits all reference to the paranoid attitudes that are characteristic of the family or culture in which the patient has grown up. And fourth, it fails to distinguish between undue expectation of harm from others, for whatever reason, and the specific attribution of their malign intent. Once we begin to explore the variety of reasons why someone may feel the world to be a more dangerous place than it actually is, we are on fertile ground. The patient may, for instance, have been so weakened by overprotection or invasion in childhood that he is incapable of coping with situations that are all in a day's work to most people. There are those who avoid situations of conflict not only out of fear of their own anger but because they lack a successful history of handling them well. I will give an example.

> Jeanette came to her session very angry with a man who was coming to live near her house, describing him as an objectionable person who did not respect one's privacy and who was apt to walk uninvited into people's gardens and behave aggressively. We discussed the situation in some detail and came to the conclusion that the extent of her anxiety and rage was out of proportion to the present predicament. I reminded Jeanette of the similarity of her current feelings to those toward her mother, who had impinged on her in a way that she found difficult to resist.
>
> At that point in the session, the window cleaner appeared, and although he finished the job in one minute flat, Jeanette, who was sitting opposite me, was visibly disturbed and admitted that her heart was thumping. Even when the cleaner had descended and could be heard in the distance talking to his mate, Jeanette was still very disturbed by his voice.
>
> It seemed that Jeanette had never learned how to cope with her mother's invasion of her privacy and could not now easily defend herself against those with whom reasoning was of no avail. She could let others be close to her only if she were sure that it would be possible, if she so desired, to persuade them to leave her alone.

To summarize, we cannot abandon theory, for our experience of the world is dependent on the concepts we develop, however elementary, in order to make sense of things. But it can have diminishing returns and impoverish our understanding, particularly in the realm of personal relationships. Once we get beyond the simple statement that defenses constitute an attempt to avoid or master unacceptable experiences, we must tread carefully. Theory can never accommodate the subtleties and nuances of human intercourse for which we require all the flexibility of ordinary language.

Chapter Eight

Dependence

Tell me where is fancy bred,
Or in the heart or in the head?
How begot, how nourished?
  Reply, reply.
It is engender'd in the eyes,
With gazing fed; and fancy dies
In the cradle where it lies.
  —William Shakespeare

One of the few assertions that can be made with confidence about child development is that the child is at first enormously dependent on those around him, primarily his mother. If what is provided falls short of his needs beyond a certain threshold, there is not much he can do about it except become psychologically impoverished or ill. He will try to compensate for what is missing in ways that ill-adapt him to the future. If, however, the needs are sufficiently met, he is ready for the next hurdle, which is to limit his dependence on his mother and rely more on others, both within and outside the family. This is a matter not only of his becoming a more competent person but of being able to relate to a wider variety of people; he still remains, and will always remain, dependent on those around him.

In order to get to grips with the question of dependence, it is important to make a distinction between needs and wishes. The distinction cannot be absolute because each of us has to decide on the threshold at which we ourselves regard the impoverishment as unacceptable or pathogenic. In extreme cases, we can be reasonably clear about this. If a child is not given sufficient protein, he will become physically incapacitated, and if he receives no meaningful communication he will become psychologically disintegrated. Such needs are what I understand

Winnicott to mean by *absolute dependence*, although I doubt whether such dependence is confined to infancy.

The child's wishes may more or less coincide with his needs or may be different, especially in degree. For example, he may want the mother around more than is necessary to sustain health. His task (like ours as therapists) is to distinguish between need and wish, or, to put it another way, to establish his rights. This task is complicated by the fact that in order to make this distinction he needs to be provided with a realistic assessment by others. He can, for example, be easily persuaded that what is a reasonable expectation is much more or much less than is really the case, that is, he can be either spoiled or deprived, with the result that he feels omnipotent or impotent. The concept of rights is a difficult one for they appear to be arbitrary—that is to say, no one but God has the wisdom to say what are the rights of a human being. In our society there is a rough and ready consensus that a child has some right to dependence and some right to autonomy, and the precise way that this is interpreted by a particular family, and even in relation to a particular child in the family, will have an enormous influence on his sense of what he may or may not expect of the world and of himself.

Most of us, unhappily, never manage to resolve the conflict of dependence sufficiently well to ensure serenity of mind, and those who come for therapy invariably bring the conflict with them in one form or another. Moreover there are differing opinions as to how adults should behave in this respect. How dependent should we be on each other, and in what way? Should we strive for self-sufficiency, stoically and silently enduring our anxieties and hiding our wounds, or should we openly share our vulnerabilities with others and turn to them for help and succor? There are clearly dangers in limiting ourselves to either strategy of living, as, for example, can be seen in the unhappy consequences of stereotypical sex roles. It would seem, in general, that psychotherapy leans in the direction of open admission of need; the very essence of the healing process is the sharing of the secret vulnerable self. And yet, in what appears to be a paradox, its declared purpose is often phrased in terms of a weaning from a persistent and unhealthy craving for a state of infantile dependence.

PSYCHOANALYTIC THEORIES
OF INFANTILE EXPERIENCE

One reason for this confusing state of affairs is, I believe, that Freud conceived the infant as a passive being who, under the influence of his instincts, strove to satisfy himself, and that Melanie Klein, who has had such immense impact on psycho-analysis, chose to follow the same path. In Klein's view, the infant sees the mother as an object to be controlled rather than as a person to relate to in complex ways. Insofar as the mother is his possession, she is not a separate being on whom he can depend except in the way that a car driver is dependent on the functioning of the gears. This view of early childhood pervades psychoanalytic thinking, and even Winnicott, who writes so imaginatively about the dependency of the baby, refers to the mother as an "object." There is no possibility of refuting this view, for we cannot ask a baby to put his experience into concepts. It would seem, however, to be a debatable one. When early experiences are repeated in the consulting room, we often find that we are dealing with quite sophisticated conceptions (such as pride, humiliation, regret, and a sense of responsibility), which are not as restricted as the theory suggests; and it is, in fact, rather difficult to feel any confidence in a precise theory of infant development on the basis of our observations.

A recognition of the extent of early dependency means that the therapist will, like the child, be concerned with the details of her patient's particular environment. The child who wishes for a real relationship with the mother, a relationship in which negotiation is possible, will need to be sensitive to her aims and states of mind and will carry his early experiences of these throughout his life. It is not enough to say that a patient suffered from early frustration or was innately constituted to intolerance of it; we have to explore with him, as best we can, the exact nature of the frustration and his response to it.

One of the features of infancy to which Klein, more than anyone else, has alerted us, is the intensity of hate of which the child is capable and the devastating and contorted consequences of this hate. Because of his fear of the results of his destructive urges toward the desired object and his reluctance to take responsibility for the results, the baby, Klein believes, projects his hate outward; it is the object that is cruel and the source of all trouble. One need not accept the Kleinian theory of infant development nor her edicts on how to conduct therapy in order to recognize that there is much validity in these formulations of defense mechanisms.

There remains, however, the question as to the source of the child's hate. Those who, unlike Klein, attribute it primarily to his reaction to environmental failure lay emphasis on the enormous support necessary to sustain the development of a self. Lack of the necessary support (and other disadvantageous factors, such as confusion, which I discuss in the next chapter) is likely to lead to a vicious circle, for the child will fail to develop completely and will become even more dependent: the weaker the child feels, the greater his anger; the greater his anger, the more disintegrated and fragile he becomes.

RESPONSES IN THERAPY TO VULNERABILITY

As a consequence of these conflicting ideas about infancy, there are (to put the matter rather crudely) two kinds of psychotherapists. The first kind is interested in the desires and vicissitudes of the child, who is held responsible if things have gone wrong; the task of the therapist is to reveal to the patient the faulty thinking that has led to his downfall. If he can understand himself better, he can then deal with life better. The second kind of therapist believes, in keeping with Freud's early trauma theory and its elaboration by Ferenczi, that the child becomes sick because the world failed him, and that he is not responsible for his sickness. The task of the therapist is to provide a setting that is different from the one that led to his undoing, a setting in which healing can take place. Neither of these imagined therapists exists in pure form, for the two ideas are not mutually exclusive. However, the difference in emphasis is a very significant one for the patient. How can we begin to decide which one is nearer the truth? My own personal thinking on the matter is something as follows.

Let us suppose that a friend is in some kind of terrible mess, and we wish to help him. First we will comfort him and give what practical aid we can. Second, we may suggest ways in which he might extricate himself from his plight. And third, particularly if the predicament seems to be one that he has brought on himself, we may encourage him to reflect on the reasons he came to make a fool of himself.

Although the psychotherapist will, I believe, often comfort and sometimes advise, his main preoccupations are with the third of these endeavors: trying to enable the patient to understand the ways in which he has failed to deal realistically and fruitfully with his life. The crucial question, however, is how best to show the other the error of his thinking. Simply pointing it out may not help. The therapist, therefore, may resort to acting in some way (a crude form of which is to shout at him) in order to shift his perspective. Long-term therapy gives the chance of consistently responding in ways likely to show him that his expectations of others are not necessarily correct, that, for example, his assumption that the therapist wishes to have complete control of his mind is a mistaken one. Moreover, if the faulty appreciation of reality occurred at an age when the capacity for thought was too undeveloped to tackle the problem, no amount of explanation or interpretation will succeed until the original emotional trauma has been surmounted. The conditions for this growth are similar to those necessary for such development in childhood and depend primarily on a safe, realistic, and unconfusing relationship with another human being. The therapist, therefore, must provide a setting that is near enough to this need to suffice; he has to decide the degree to which the total therapeutic response—the provision of a new experience—is necessary, quite apart from any intellectual insight that might be gained from interpretation. This decision, and the thinking that lies behind it, is, I believe, central to the practice of psychotherapy and lies at the heart of the famous conflict between Freud and Ferenczi, including the question of the relative merits of remembering the past through reconstruction or reliving past experience in the analytic situation, and of the respective values of abstinence and responsiveness (Hoffer 1991). Ferenczi was given a hard time by his colleagues for his ideas (Roazen 1975). His clinical diaries, written in 1932, were not translated into English until 1988 (see Ferenczi 1988). We are now able to appreciate the richness of his thinking and the ways in which he anticipated the writings of Winnicott and Balint, which, in more recent years, have had a powerful influence on our ideas of dependence in therapy.

Winnicott did not openly challenge the classical method of

interpretation but focused his attention on certain very disturbed patients—sometimes called "schizoid" or "borderline"—for whom, he maintained, orthodox psychoanalysis was inadequate because they needed a special response. In his view, some patients have to regress to a state of extreme dependence, in which their sense of themselves is so lost that they need to be "held" by the therapist, as, for example, a baby needs to be held by its mother. Winnicott also believes that what is being experienced at this time is a repetition of a breakdown that occurred in infancy. He formulates the matter as follows (the language I use is not necessarily quite the same as Winnicott's).

The environment so fails certain children that they are unable to continue proper growth and remain frozen at a certain point in time. The *true self*—the core of healthy growth—is repressed and tucked safely away in the hope that one day conditions may be sufficiently favorable for it to emerge again. In the meantime, life in the world continues on the basis of a *false self*, which adapts to society as best as it can, concealing and contradicting the true self, nervously controlling events by maneuvers of various kinds, gaining comfort from the presentation of a persona that, at least, is not totally rejected and, at best, shines forth before the world as an admirable example of the way to live.

When such a person enters therapy, he does all he can to conceal the true self, deceptively and ingeniously adapting to the therapy as he has adapted to society. If, however, the therapist can help him to understand the concealment and engage his trust, then he may be able to organize a breakdown through which growth can occur.

The breakdown brings terror and helplessness, and the therapist is called upon to give more support to the patient than is usual in therapy, which, in extreme cases, might even involve making arrangements for him to be looked after between sessions. Winnicott uses the word *holding* to describe this response but does not imply that it *necessarily* includes a physical support of the patient. Elsewhere I (Lomas 1973) have described such a happening, one feature of which was the notable efforts of the patient to attack the false self's attempt to regain its ground and get back to business as usual. A dream may help to illustrate the state of mind of a patient who is experiencing a regression.

"I was standing on the bank of a dark, muddy lake. On the other side of the lake was a girl, about 5 years old, in distress. There was a group of people near to me who, although responsible for the girl, didn't appear to see her and walked away. At this point the girl gestured, and I made a responsive gesture back. She then, to my horror, jumped into the water. I knew she couldn't swim, and I knew I had to plunge in although I myself am a weak swimmer. But it was easier than I had expected. I reached the girl and managed to keep her head above water. A rowing boat was nearby on the lake, and we struggled into it and lay down wet and exhausted. The sun came out and dried us, and the boat drifted back to the shore. The people returned, had no idea what had happened, and seemed rather amazed."

Winnicott's image of regression to dependence is one of the most powerful and poignant to have emerged from psychotherapy and has had a profound influence on many practitioners, including myself. Indeed, if I were asked to discard all the writings since Freud, these would probably be the last to go. However, there is a danger. Our tendency to idealize a creative thinker is almost boundless, and Winnicott, in emphasizing the enormous sensitivity and vast experience required to handle such a very special and delicate situation, colludes with this tendency, filling us with awe and inhibiting our critical faculties. Much of psychotherapy requires the best in us in courage, sensitivity, and wisdom, and, to select regression as a phenomenon that requires a quite special category of response is, I believe, to do injustice to the intuition gained in the ordinary course of living.

Recently, a therapist who is early in her career came to me for supervision and described a patient whom she is seeing, against her usual practice, five times a week. He lies on the couch but insists on facing the therapist, and their eyes meet over long periods. Almost everything that happens feels to the therapist as though a baby is searching out and dependent on his mother's gaze. The patient manages to maintain his life between sessions. At the end of the sessions, although finding it difficult to leave, he expresses his deep gratitude to the therapist, who, despite feeling in her heart that she is responding in a healing way and the only way she can, looks at me for reassurance and asks, "Is it all right?" I believe it is. This is not to deny that the therapist finds the task a great strain. (Indeed, one of her queries was the amount to which it might be safe to admit to this man who scrutinized her so intensely that it *was* a strain.) But although more experience would probably lessen the strain, there are other factors that bear upon the matter: the capacity of the therapist, as a person, to cope with the dependence of others, and what happens to be going on in his or her life outside the consulting room.

To return, however, to the question as to how dependence is best conceived as an intrinsic aspect of therapy, I wish to suggest that the distinction that Winnicott makes between ordinary therapy and holding, and between people with false selves and those without, is too strict. We cannot divide these into sheep or goats. In most therapies, there is quite a bit of holding, and limited breakdowns occur from time to time. And even when severe regression occurs, we do not stop trying to help the patient understand what is happening. To put the matter another way, there is no such thing as a pure regression to dependence in which the patient is conflict-free and can simply trust and allow himself to be comforted and healed. We should not expect this, for the state is a complex one. Certainly there are moments, as in ordinary life, when we feel in the presence of someone who is at that moment fully and authentically open, loving, and trusting, but the ongoing regression contains many elements other than this happy one. In respect of dependence, therefore, the psychotherapeutic encounter is best conceived as existing in a continuum, in which the regressed patient provides an example of one extreme.

Because the patient has lost his way and needs help, the therapeutic relationship is inherently a dependent one. The issue of his reliance on the therapist is pervasive and dominant; all the difficulties he has experienced during his life in allowing himself to trust others are likely to reappear in therapy, for he has been placed in a position guaranteed to awaken his deepest traumas and to severely test his shaky confidence in the world. The drama of this situation is primarily formulated by psychoanalysis in terms of transference. The task of the therapist is to interpret these conflicts and to be sufficiently reliable to enable the patient to trust her enough to listen to her interpretations. But (and this is where I find myself in sympathy with Ferenczi and those who emphasize the healing power of the relationship per se) during the whole process, from beginning to end, what is most conducive to growth is the *way* in which the therapist relates to her patient.

This kind of commitment—that which depends on the authentic feelings of the therapist—is likely to be the subject of the patient's deepest doubt, cynicism, and his resistance to exposing his vulnerability. He can easily use the fact that the contract is a professional one as a reason for ridiculing the idea that dependence on the genuine goodwill of the therapist is conceivable. This kind of argument can be put in a very plausible way, and the therapist may well find herself asking the

question, "Am I really justified in looking for hidden dependence? Why should the patient give his heart to someone who
demands to be paid and turns him out after 50 minutes? How
arrogant of me!" Such misgivings are understandable and show
a healthy measure of humility but can easily be given too much
weight, for the therapist usually feels an emotional commitment
that transcends the contract, and, in any case, the point is to
recognize that the dependent feelings exist whether they are
appropriate or based on illusion. Moreover, the therapist may be
tempted, for her own psychic well-being, to deny that she is
faced with a dependency of frightening intensity that she can
never fully satisfy.

The handling of dependence in therapy is as difficult, if not
more so, as the handling by parents of their children's dependence. One can so easily get it wrong. It is in the area of the
extreme case that creative work has been done, notably by
Michael Balint (1968). Balint divides regression into two kinds:
benign and *malignant*. Once again we must beware of a too neat
formulation that depicts people and states of mind as either
black or white. Nevertheless, Balint calls our attention most
usefully to the negative aspects of the phenomenon.

The benign type of regression takes the form described by
Winnicott and is therapeutically beneficial. In the malignant
form, by contrast, the condition becomes an addiction, and the
patient's demands increase to the point of insatiability. A folie à
deux can easily develop, in which the more the therapist tries to
adapt to her patient's "needs," the more helpless and demanding
he becomes. There is a hysterical flavor to the behavior of these
patients, and they appear to derive a sense of identity from their
"illness" – a phenomenon that I discuss in more detail in Chapter
13. One factor that Balint does not mention, but which seems to
be of crucial importance, is that the patient may seek a solution
to the problem by abandoning his true self and giving himself

over entirely to the powerful therapist, through whom he thereafter lives vicariously. This is a masochistic move by means of which he allows himself to be seduced by the power, persuasiveness, protectiveness, and charm of the therapist. The dream of a man who was in a state of crisis may help to illustrate this point.

"I was amongst a large number of people and was feeling terribly angry. I went round destroying things, and everyone was dismayed by this. At one point I got hold of a valuable Rolls Royce, took it to the middle of a field, and was about to break it up. It was suggested that someone should be asked to reason with me. I saw, amongst the crowd, a clergyman whom I admire and like despite our differing views on religion. I thought, 'It's going to be him.' And sure enough, it was. I said to myself, 'Oh! No!' He came up and said, 'Perhaps you just want someone to put their arms round you and kiss you.' These words took away my anger and I thanked him. But I was uneasy for some reason." In recounting the dream, the patient said that the saying "to kill with kindness" came into his head.

It is tempting to think of an apparently insatiable patient as merely greedy, but the driving force behind such behavior usually stems, I believe, from a terror of annihilation causing him to seek alternative gratifications as a compensation for his impoverished state or in the vain hope that these might really turn out to provide the answer to his anguish. In such a situation, distinctions between true and false selves, benign and malignant regressions, or pre-oedipal and oedipal states of mind often become blurred. The patient is confused as to what he really needs, and anyone who tries to help him is in danger of becoming embroiled in this confusion.

The question as to whether orthodox psychoanalytic technique induces a crippling dependency was forcefully considered in Ferenczi. In his clinical diary, he wrote: "The analytic situation, but specifically its rigid technical rules, mostly produce in the patient an unalleviated suffering and in the analyst an unjustifiable sense of superiority accompanied by a certain contempt for the patient" (quoted in Roazen 1990, p. 370).

In order to understand how analytic thinking could make the mistake of reducing the patient to the states of mind described by Ferenczi, we have to make a distinction between dependence and passivity. It is increasingly recognized by developmental psychology that although the infant is dependent, he is by no means passive. In a healthy situation, there is a living interchange between mother and baby in which both partners are changed by each other; there is negotiation. The baby can, of course, be made passive if the mother is not responsive. This kind of problem remains the case throughout childhood; the child may be allowed an identity by his family, or one may be thrust upon him. The frequency with which an identity is imposed on a child plays a part, I believe, in the passivity and defensive withdrawal of so many of our patients. It may also have a bearing on the bleak theories, prevalent in contemporary thought, that center on the idea that we have no self and are merely the product of society and language. It is a pity that Erikson, who is so creative in describing the vicissitudes of a sense of identity (Erickson 1968), has to a large extent gone out of fashion.

For these kinds of reasons, therapists need to ensure that their relationship with patients is a two-way process in which both participants can express their individuality and negotiate their rights. The idea that therapy is a technique that can be imposed on the patient rather than a mutual exploration can easily reinforce the original pressure toward passivity, which is so central to most of the problems that patients bring. Therefore, holding the regressed patient must always involve a recognition of and response to his active and responsible striving to change us.

To achieve a healthy degree of mutuality, insofar as is possible, does not of course eliminate the problem of dependence in therapy. This is not only because, as I have suggested, simply turning for help engenders dependent feelings but because prolonged closeness creates desires on both sides. And, as in ordinary life, to strike a happy balance between intimacy and limitation is an art that is beyond most of us.

Although the degree to which those in misfortune should be helped or left to dig themselves out of trouble is a subject that is open to debate, it would seem that an appropriate word to describe our present society's attitude to this matter is *paranoid*. We cannot trust that we will be cared for if we fall by the wayside, and so, with the bitterness of the paranoid attitude, we look after ourselves rather than others. But responsibility has, to an extent, crept in by the back door, and the growth of counseling and therapy is one manifestation. The professional, rather than the neighbor, is now the person to whom we must turn, resulting in what Chabot (1979) refers to as "the erosion of the right to care for each other." Despite the fact that the danger to which Chabot refers is a real one, we cannot expect the healing of some wounds to take place except in the privileged context of the therapy. Moreover, the insights gained in this set-up help us to recognize and perhaps make some impact upon the prevalent denial of the human need for dependence at all stages of the life cycle.

Chapter Nine

Confusion

It is this deep blankness is the real thing strange
The more things happen to you the more you can't
Tell or remember even what they were.

The contradictions cover such a range
The talk would talk and go so far aslant
You don't want madhouse and the whole thing there.

— William Empson

The child fails to learn reality if it is so unacceptable to her that she denies it or if it is presented in a distorted and confusing way. Freud emphasized the former. The desires of the child, he maintained, are of such magnitude that the world is bound to disappoint her. She attempts to bridge the gap by creating illusion and repressing her urges; and unless a satisfactory accommodation can be made, she falls ill. The illness takes the form of symptoms—or a disorder of personality—which are an unhappy compromise between desire and the forces of repression. Symptoms, Freud believed, are expressed in the language of the unconscious. Despite the many modifications of theory that have been introduced, Freud's basic thesis still dominates psychoanalytic thought, and those of us who daily attempt to understand the meaning of symptoms owe an enormous debt to his formulations with which we can hope to unravel indirect communications. As I suggested earlier, this does not mean that the therapist need be a theoretician to understand dreams and symptoms; with a little guidance and confidence many people have a remarkably intuitive grasp of unconscious functioning.

SEXUALITY

In discussing the matter of coming to terms with reality, Freud placed special emphasis on sexuality. The degree to which he believed that the vicissitudes of the sexual drive are responsible for our illnesses has met with a great deal of criticism. It is, as Jung was quick to realize, a reductive theory that does disservice to the complexity of human beings. Moreover, Freud did not take into account the cultural factor: late nineteenth-century Vienna was sexually a more guilt-ridden society than our own, and the symptoms shown by many of his "hysterical" patients are uncommon today. Despite these and many other justified criticisms of such emphasis, sexuality is unquestionably a central issue in health, and Freud's ideas remain powerful ones. He believed that the most unacceptable piece of reality that confronts every child is that the parent whom she adores belongs to another. One does not have to be a therapist to recognize, from observations of family life, the force of this belief; it is clear that children find it acutely painful when their loved parent turns to someone else, and they are readily consumed with jealousy by this occurrence. But Freud went further. The child, he maintained, experiences passionate genital desire for the parent and harbors murderous wishes toward her rival.

The degree to which children are preoccupied with this kind of oedipal wish is debatable. According to Freud, it is universal, stereotyped, and dictates the child's adjustment to reality. The boy accepts the limitation of his aims only under the imagined threat of castration by the father. (Freud's theory of the comparable conflict in the girl is complicated by the fact that, for him, castration denotes the destruction of the *male* genital, a view that is, in part, a consequence of his patriarchal attitude.)

That castration anxiety can clearly be seen in many patients today is undeniable. Usually it occurs in symbolic form—in fears of illness, death, amputation, and so on—and we can only infer its presence, bearing in mind the danger that we may impose our theory on data that do not sufficiently support it, forgetting, for example, the universal fear of death and its widespread denial. Sometimes, however, the fear of castration is manifest. I will give an example.

A young man had dreams and fantasies in which he was physically castrated: either there was a gap where his genitals should be, or they were being attacked by a knife. These fantasies were intensely vivid and painful, and he would sometimes appear to be in anguish as he shrank into himself and covered his genitals with his hands.

One night he had two dreams. In the first, he was walking about the house, at night, and had a huge erection. In the second, he was driving his car. He got out at one point to look at his map. When he turned round, the car was running out of control, and he realized that he had left the brake off. Fortunately the car, although still out of control, went into a field. He chased after it only to discover that the field contained an enormous and fierce bull attempting to charge at him but was restrained by a rope that didn't look very secure. He was terrified.

The dream shows, I believe, the masculine, aggressive, and sexual urges that underlie his castration anxiety. Such urges are a terrible threat to him. But one reality that he must face is the existence of these urges, and my task as a therapist is to help him confront and accept them. This is the kind of conflict that Freud had in mind when he considered the ways in which we turn away from reality.

We do, however, need to be cautious. Although, in this instance as in many others, there was little doubt as to the sexual nature of the symptoms, we cannot assume that this is all there

is to the matter. Sexuality may indeed be a symbol of something
else. The genitals may represent the vitality of living. The bull in
the dream could stand for pent-up aggression. And castration
could symbolize the failure of active development and consequent weakness and passivity.

THE INFLUENCE OF THE FAMILY

Despite the force of Freud's argument, it would seem that his
enthusiasm led him too far from an obvious reason for a child's
failure to form a realistic perception of the world. In childhood,
we are at the mercy of the views of those around us. Long before
she speaks, the parents respond to the child in ways that are
bound to have a profound influence on her, not the least on her
view of herself. They may behave in a very casual, indifferent
manner, or they may react to her gestures with delight, alarm,
surprise, or repugnance. And when talk begins, these impressions will be modified into conceptions: she is lovable or unlovable; she is unimportant; she is a nuisance, even dangerous; she
is coherent or chaotic, and so on. How can she possibly view
herself without reference to these responses? How can she match
them with her own perceptions of herself, the world of the
home, and later, the world outside the home? I will give an
example of a man who could remember his childhood rather
well.

> Mark was in his mid-fifties and had periods of therapy at
> several points in his life. In what follows, I shall focus on the
> impact of his family upon him rather than the reasons for
> their behavior and his own impact upon them.

The family was very united, loyal, loving, respectably middle-class, and held in high regard by others. Mark was the youngest of three children, both of his sisters being appreciably older. He was doted upon and overprotected. His life seemed to him to be in the control of others. His bowel movements were monitored and inspected, and he was nightly dosed with a purgative; if his function departed from what was regarded as the norm, he was given an enema. He slept in his mother's bed until the age of 8 and in her room until 12. If he developed a cold, the doctor was summoned, and he was confined to bed for several days, whatever the doctor's suggestions on the matter. Until around the age of 8 or so, he was allowed to play with only one or two carefully selected children and, for the most part, was never allowed out of the garden. Invitations to parties were turned down by the parents.

It is hardly surprising that Mark should have been tormented by dreams and fantasies of being suffocated, strangled, bound, hypnotized, stuck in an underground cave or tunnel, or dead. In one fantasy, he was buried alive or in some way rendered without speech, sight, hearing, or movement. His greatest dread, however, was that he would be thought mad and sent to a "lunatic asylum."

The fear of madness was, I believe, a measure of his inability to grasp reality. He knew intuitively that something was terribly wrong; the world, at times, felt utterly remote and alien. Yet what *could* be wrong? His family were loving people whose actions all made sense and were justified by convincing arguments and who were respected by friends and neighbors. It must have been puzzling, however, to discover, on the occasions when he came into contact with other families, that their behavior was significantly different in ways that were alarming yet provoked in him a yearning to be more like them.

The division between family and outer world was not clear-cut. Mark's parents were not cold fish, entirely preoccupied with caution and control. They were warm and capable of passion and revered the romantic poets and the novels of Walter Scott and the Brontës; the sources of imagination were by no means confined to the outer world. In the midst of this confusion, Mark had enormous difficulty in developing a stable idea of how one should live and could never come to terms with the concept of risk. Central to this dilemma was his sense of sexual identity. In many ways he was treated like a girl. His father was ineffectual within the household—a failure for which Mark never forgave him—thus ensuring that a happy identification with a male eluded his grasp.

The traumatic impact of Mark's environment was unspectacular but is well conveyed by his memory of an afternoon—and, indeed, a seemingly endless series of afternoons—in winter, in the drawing room, looking out through the window. His father was at work. His sisters were at school, and his mother was upstairs taking her afternoon nap. The grandfather clock was ticking in the hall. He was not allowed outside. Perhaps he had a slight cold or was recovering from one. Perhaps the weather was unfavorable. He was bored—endlessly, insufferably bored. He was not aware of anger but of a kind of dread. Soon the boys and girls would be coming home from the state school, and he would hear their shouting or laughing as they went by. After tea, in the late afternoon or early evening, he would be put to bed lovingly and read a story. His father may look in when he came home, give him a cuddle, say a few words, and go down for supper. But Mark would lie awake, either because he was not tired enough for sleep or because he was afraid that if he slept he might die. If, in his anguish, he cried out for his parents, they would come upstairs in order to comfort him, but it was a task beyond their capacity.

There is no proof that Mark's memory of his childhood is a true record, but there is rarely proof of anything that our patients tell us, and I have no reason to doubt his vivid and poignant account. The point I wish to make is that he needed to recall the experience and to share it in a way in which the therapist listened with respect and without too much cynicism; and that to do this brought him, if only a little way, toward a sense of the reality of living. Without that reality, we have no way of assessing appropriate feelings and actions, for much that we learn is culturally conveyed. Mark experienced a terrifying hate of the world but did not know whether it was justified or not, and in his confusion, he repressed it, only to be haunted by fantasies that unknowingly he had killed someone, or that he would suddenly discover that everyone in the world was dead. Although it is valuable, even essential, for the therapist to unveil the patient's hidden fury, it is, I believe, useful to do so only if the reasons for the fury can be identified in the actual experience of the child. With this proviso, it is, however, a necessary part of unraveling confusion to pursue the ways in which the child complicates experience in the interests of defense. One of the many insights Freud has passed on to us is the way in which the tormented struggles of the child to find some degree of peace, safety, and satisfaction lead to dissociation and confusion. In order to preserve some goodness in her world, the child will deny painful experiences (deprivations, loss, threat, rage, even confusion itself) only to find that they return in distorted forms, such as obsessional doubt, the prototype of which may be the question, "Do I *really* love my parents or not?" One confusing occurrence is the fact that she may be stricter on herself than her parents ever were. How does this come about? Let us look at some of the self-destructive fantasies that were to be found in the patient described above.

> I will pretend that I enjoy deprivation or that I believe it to be a worthier way of living than the pleasure-seekers.
>
> By exaggerating the strictness of my parents, I will show them up and make them regret their behavior.
>
> If I punish myself first, I avoid the shock and humiliation of parental punishment.
>
> I am frightened of the enormity of my desires and my aggression, and I must crush them.
>
> I cannot stand the pain of living; I will (psychically) annihilate myself.
>
> I will do penance and thus avert punishment and lessen guilt.
>
> I will give up all my own hopes and live through another who is, unlike me, fine and perfect.
>
> It is safer to vent my fury on myself than on anyone else, and I will be savage with myself in the ways that I have learned from others.

The confusions that result from defensive thinking, which are so difficult to unravel in therapy, were described by Freud in terms of the oedipal triangle; Melanie Klein, among others, has increased our understanding of them, depicting the conflict in terms of the infant's relation to her mother's breast. We do not necessarily need to locate the inevitable origins of pathology in the areas favored by Freud and Klein or accept the idea that the complexities that occupied them are those that are relevant to any particular patient; their main use lies in their description of ways in which people may distort reality in the service of psychic survival. However, Klein's assumptions that the defensive mechanisms of the child are the most significant feature of a confused and distorted view of reality led her to neglect the overwhelming impact of the environment and to recommend an interpretative kind of therapy, which does injustice to the child's perceptual capacity and may well reinforce the original trauma. We have to turn to Ferenczi, and later to Winnicott, to find, in psychoanalytic thought, a sense of the child's vulnerability to external forces. Alice Miller (1983), who finally renounced the profession of psychoanalysis, has written movingly and convincingly of the external traumas of childhood, but unfortunately she overstates an otherwise good case by appearing to believe that all analysts ignore the historical reality of their patients' lives, and that all parents are blindly insensitive to the real needs of their children.

The confusing atmosphere of childhood can quite suddenly be recaptured by incidents that in themselves are of no great moment. Jane described to me a social occasion when a woman spoke about the near-death experiences in which people have a sense of almost entering a kind of heavenly world. Such accounts, the woman maintained, were sufficient evidence to abolish the fear of death. All those present agreed with her, except Jane, who believed that the woman was denying the existence of her fear. Jane was extremely disturbed by this conversation; she felt alone, mad, threatened, and trampled upon. It was clearly an overreaction.

As we talked about the conversation, Jane was reminded of the fact that there had been a death in her family when she was a small child. Although the death was acknowledged as a fact, its significance was not; there was a pretense that all was well, and Jane recalled that the same feelings of confusion, threat, and madness that she had experienced the previous evening were there as a child. Her sense of reality had again been seriously challenged. It was no coincidence, I think, that Jane was creative in her work yet terrified of her creativity. Creativity involves a thought that goes beyond the generally accepted, provokes anxiety in others, and tests the security of one's own perceptions.

THE QUESTION OF AMBIGUITY

Approaching the question of childhood confusion from a quite different position, a number of American workers, of whom the most significant was Gregory Bateson, studied communication in the families of schizophrenic patients. Bateson's thesis (1973) is that children become traumatically confused when a parent gives them a message that is expressed in two different and contradictory forms of expression. For example, a mother may say, "Oh! No! I'm not angry at all! How could you think that?" while at the same time her eyes and her gestures convey a controlled fury. The child's predicament, which Bateson referred to as a *double-bind*, is that he has no means of responding coherently, no way of understanding or stating his dilemma, and no escape. One weakness of this theory is the fact that such unfortunate failures of communication are so common as to be part of daily living, yet they do not necessarily appear to result in severe illness; but this apparent discrepancy could no doubt be explained in terms of the intensity of the denial and confusion to which a particular child is subjected.

A more far-reaching difficulty with the theory is that it is not necessarily harmful to a child if reality is presented to her in terms that are ambiguous (Lomas 1981). Because existence is not neatly definable but is unknown and mysterious, it would in fact be misleading to present it in rigid terms. In a healthy, tolerant, and non-obsessional family, this fact is accepted, and the ambiguities of life are conveyed in play and humor; the words of the parent can be realistically interpreted by the child in the context of the relationship and particular situation, and the ambiguities and discrepancies of communication that are bound to occur will not undermine her position. She can rest secure in the knowledge that the parents have sufficient love and understanding to look after her adequately.

In trying to learn about reality, the child not only is up against contradictory messages from a parent but has to decide whether the reality that is presented to her is a true one. By this I mean not only simple statements of fact (e.g., "the pillar box is red," "the man next door has three cats") but questions of morality and custom (e.g., "little girls don't play rough games"). It would seem that the task of the parent is to present a world that not only is coherently communicated but is sufficiently near the practical facts and psychological reality and presents them in a way that takes cognizance of the mores of the culture.

I have said little in this chapter about the therapeutic response to confusion, but I have tried to make clear throughout this book my belief that the task of the therapist is not merely to point out and interpret confusion but to counteract it by ensuring that he is as straightforward and unconfusing in the room as can possibly be managed. I hope that the above discussion gives some indication of why such a stance is important.

Chapter Ten

Seduction

Goethe smiled and said the following fateful words to the young woman: "You are a charming child." As soon as she heard the word "child" she lost all shyness. She announced that she was uncomfortable on the couch and jumped to her feet. "Sit down where you feel comfortable" said Goethe and Bettina sat on his lap and hugged him.

—Milan Kundera "Immortality"

The fear of seduction is one of the deepest forces of behavior in people, and the distinction between benign and malignant attempts to influence the other is a crucial one. By means of encouragement, warmth, and tact, by behaving with qualities that are harmonious and aesthetically pleasing, by our tones of voice and gestures and adaptations, we give enjoyment to others and make it likely that they will desire our company and listen to what we have to say.

As psychotherapists, we need our patients to trust us, to listen to us, and perhaps to have loving feelings toward us in order that we may influence and have a fruitful relationship with them. But how do we distinguish between behavior that will fruitfully engender this desirable result and that which is seductive? There are, I believe, no hard and fast rules to guide us along this precarious path. Success depends on our capacity to respect the patient's autonomy and point of view while in the process of encouraging him to entertain the idea of a new, and perhaps more hazardous, way of being. We must also be on the alert for signs that the patient is a potential victim for seduction. When it is clear that he is attempting to be conformist, self-effacing, effusive, or ingratiating, it is not usually difficult to recognize his painful need to be accepted at all costs.

The danger of being seduced is not, of course, confined to the patient. Although the therapist may abuse his position of power, he is also under threat from the subtle strivings of the more dependent partner to undermine his authority and destroy his therapeutic capacity. This danger is increased by the fact that in order to take full cognizance of the patient's predicament, he needs to suspend the cynicism that protects one from false enchantment. The more difficult engagements are those with whom we find we have an intuitive bond, who appeal to us without our knowing wherein the magic lies, and whose demeanor gives all the signs of genuine warmth and love and consideration for us. To interpret this as seduction may be to make a terrible blunder—to destroy the stirrings of long-dead feelings of love evoked by the situation and perhaps even by a genuine appreciation of what we are as therapists and as persons. And yet such are the tumultuous feelings in the patient, and such is the hypnotic power of the transference, that an authentic loving may be corrupted by a desperate and ruthlessly seductive desire to take possession of the therapist at all costs, or by a bitterness and hate at a felt rejection that will be satisfied only by the evil destruction of the therapist's integrity and apparent unassailability.

In this predicament, the therapist has all kinds of self-preservation devices at his disposal. The best—and, of course, the first in the history of psychotherapy—is the concept of transference. This may save the sanity not only of the patient but of the therapist as well. By means of the concept, he can regard the protestations of his patient as something that has nothing directly to do with him, as, for example, calculated and devious strategies to possess and undermine the parent for whom he stands. The heat is then off. However correct such interpretations may be, if used primarily in the interests of non-engagement or as a routine way of thinking, they may easily be seen by the patient as a rejection of his or her deepest emotions. Moreover, the therapist who interprets sexual feelings toward him as the reemergence of childhood devotion to a parent may infantilize the patient, thereby reinforcing those inner and outer inhibitions against his emergence as a sexual being. The patient may bring his own contribution to this predicament, presenting his craving for the therapist in infantile ways, thereby encouraging the therapist to view them as primitive rather than adult sexual needs.

THE RESPONSIBILITY FOR SEDUCTION IN THERAPY

Who is responsible for seduction in therapy? Traditionally, as passed down from the medical profession, it is the practitioner, assumed to be male, who abuses the patient, assumed to be female. The thinking behind this comes from several sources: doctors usually were male, and there was an assumption that, since homosexual ways were unthinkable, the victim was a woman. Moreover, the man has the physical capacity to penetrate a woman and sometimes the desire and the strength to do this against her will. And women, conceived of as passive creatures with little sexual urges of their own and even as possessions of their husbands, were seen as needing protection both as human beings and as property.

Times have changed, and women no longer are seen or see themselves in the same way. Nevertheless, despite the fact that women therapists do sometimes have sex with their patients, evidence suggests that the majority of therapists who have sex with patients are male. The complex reasons for this state of affairs involve the power relationship between the sexes in society and the ways in which men and women exploit each other, a subject that would take us too far from the specific area of therapy. Leaving aside this matter, which has been extensively explored in feminist literature, let us look at the question of responsibility.

The therapist is in a position of formidable power. He has been approached by someone in a vulnerable and relatively helpless state, seeking a person of wisdom, authority, and perhaps even magical capability. The transference illusion that is likely to develop, despite all the patient's mistrust of people left by the scars of previous encounters, is one of idealization, in which the therapist is, like the loved one, given the benefit of all doubts. The patient is primed for seduction, and the temptation for the therapist is great. Exploitation of the patient's vulnerability may take many forms, of which moral and intellectual domination is probably the most insidious, but the therapist's wish and capacity to be admired and loved and to be responded to sexually is also impressive, and the responsibility to withstand the temptation to indulge himself at the expense of the patient's autonomy is a heavy one. I doubt if any of us completely manage it.

Has the patient herself any responsibility in this respect? I think that inevitably she has. However sick we are, in whatever circumstances we are placed, we are still responsible for what we do, and this includes even the therapeutic situation. But the fact that the patient is, by definition, in a disturbed state, and in a situation that encourages the full flowering of this disturbance, must lead us to view any destructive or stupid actions on her part with extreme forbearance.

THE HEALING POWER OF LOVE

The temptations of mutual seduction are immensely complicated by the potentially healing power of love in the therapeutic situation. One of the earliest, most courageous, and most sensitive of those therapists who have emphasized the significance of the practitioner's genuine love for his patient is Ferenczi (1988). But despite the harsh criticism Ferenczi met from Freud and the psychoanalytic establishment, similar views have continued to emerge, presented by thinkers of high caliber, not least the ever-neglected Ian Suttie (1988).

That love should heal is hardly a new or surprising idea. In ordinary living, we think that things go better if love, rather than hate, is around, and psychotherapists work hard with families in the belief that children are more likely to develop and flourish if they are loved. One of the difficulties in the way of accepting the importance of the therapist's love for his patient is, I think, an understandable determination to avoid an easy sentimentality, a narcissistic overestimation of one's capacity to love, a denial of hate, or an oversimplification of an enormously complex process. I suspect that, as Halmos has lucidly argued (1965), most therapists at heart believe that their love is healing and are enriched and strengthened when this appears to be the case and the patient responds with gratitude. We have to ask, however, in what ways can this love be corrupted or revealed unwisely, leading to a harmful seduction? For the purposes of this discussion, I leave aside the ruthless and delinquent therapist who has no scruples about exploiting his patient sexually or otherwise. In this complicated situation, two features come to mind.

First, most obviously, the sheer power of his passionate feelings may override the therapist's considered judgment. In other words, love of this kind may wreak the same kind of havoc that it does elsewhere in social life. When this occurs, the therapist is vulnerable to the conviction (which may be quite erroneous) that to manifest his love in whatever form is in the best interests of the patient.

Second, and in no way in conflict with the former, the therapist may narcissistically view his love for patients as a special healing gift. The charismatic healer, the guru, who has a seductive, hypnotic power over his patients and acolytes, does so in part because he believes he is a savior. And his ministrations are by no means always confined to the spiritual and respectable. But may the ordinary practitioner have similar, if less potent, fantasies about himself? Among the several practitioners who have been in therapy with me, both men and women, and who, despite being responsible and caring people, have had sexual relations with patients, there was one man whose fantasies about himself as a healer quite clearly extended to his physical sexuality. For obvious reasons, I cannot describe these occurrences in detail.

THE REAPPEARANCE OF SEDUCTION IN CHILDHOOD

One of the most devastating effects of childhood seduction is confusion, as Ferenczi was perhaps the first to recognize. The child has no way of understanding what is happening. Not only are there no guidelines to follow, but the event is wrapped in guilt and mystification. She doubts her perception of what is going on, usually keeps it to herself, and if she tries to share it, is disbelieved. Moreover, she may well have a genuine love, even adoration, of the person who appears to be abusing her.

The same confusion can easily occur in psychotherapy and ironically and sadly is likely to occur in those very cases in which childhood seduction has taken place, for the patient repeats, and either fantasizes or actually seduces the therapist to repeat, the original trauma. The damage done when this happens does not necessarily involve sexual intercourse. I will give an example.

Petra came to me after several years of therapy, which she had ended abruptly and which had left her in a despairing and regressed state, spending much of her time lying curled up in bed. She had to be persuaded to come to see me by a friend who drove her the fifty miles from London to make the consultation possible. Her overwhelming need during the first year with me was to understand what had gone wrong with the previous therapy, of which she was able to give a clear and, apparently, remarkably balanced account, with little of the self-justifying explanations that are so tempting when reassessing a failed relationship.

It was clearly important to Petra that I gain as accurate a picture as possible of her previous therapy, and this task caused me quite a bit of soul-searching. The patients who come to us having previously been in therapy often do so because the undertaking has, to a varying degree, failed. In these circumstances, it is all too easy to criticize the earlier therapy and to complacently believe that we would have done a better job. It is, I think, partly for this reason that practitioners are reluctant to write about their therapeutic predecessors, fearing that they might be thought arrogant, disloyal to a colleague, or to have naively accepted the patient's biased version. However, despite these problems, we do sometimes need to construct a picture of what happened in a past attempt at healing in order to learn from it. Moreover, the difficulties of making such an assessment are not, I believe, inherently different from those we face when trying to reconstruct a childhood or marriage in the absence of key witnesses. In this case, I had little option but to give much time and thought to what had occurred in the therapy. As far as I could ascertain, the following took place.

Petra and her therapist were mutually attracted from the start and became fond of each other. Although Petra longed for his embrace, she reacted to any demonstration of warmth with terror and rejection and was unaware of any seductiveness on her side. The therapist, it would seem, acted for the most part in a restrained manner and spoke without emotional intonation, revealing as little as possible about his state of mind and confining himself to interpretations. However, at times (usually at the end of a session) his loving feelings came through in words and gestures of great intensity, which he never openly acknowledged during the ordinary course of the work. Petra became increasingly confused by the ambiguity of the situation, a predicament to which (as will become clear later) she was very vulnerable and which, I think, accounted for her subsequent loss of a sense of identity.

At first, Petra appeared so timid that she could hardly bring herself to come into my room, but she looked at me with a kind of hopeful trust that immediately won my heart. As our meetings progressed, I experienced an enormous need to console her by saying warm things (which I actually felt) and to reassure her that I had no sexual or predatory designs on her. I knew, however, from what she had told me of previous encounters with men that any protestations of warmth would be met by coldness and triumphant contempt, presumably because she felt that she had provoked a response that was valueless and merely a measure of the man's weakness. And, in the light of her previous therapy, I knew that the boundaries between us must be very clear. I was glad that I was her second therapist. I felt like a golfer who watches his opponent tee off and, having failed to allow for a deceptive side wind, ends up in the water. I was determined not to end up in the water.

But there were difficulties in knowing what stance to take. If I were too careful, we would never achieve the intimacy that was necessary for healing. Yet any suggestion of warmth frightened her, and she retreated. Moreover, I was determined to be as honest and open with her as I could in order to avoid the kind of double-bind that had occurred in her earlier therapy, and such openness would surely include my attraction to her. I felt I was walking a tightrope.

To what extent, I wondered, was I being seduced? To what extent were we colluding in a mutual seduction? How does one distinguish a genuine liking from a mere response to subtle manipulation? I shared my countertransference predicament with her. Petra seemed as unaware of any attempt to behave seductively to me as she had been with her previous therapist and, in fact, bemoaned her incapacity to be as sexually forthcoming as many women she knew. It gradually emerged, however, that she was indeed very afraid of her subtle power. On one occasion, for example, she was speaking to a woman whose husband she had not met and was unlikely to ever meet. Yet she felt uneasy in her presence because she was aware of a fantasy that she might steal the woman's husband.

During therapy, Petra had the following dream:

"I was in a session with you, but the room was extraordinarily long. We were sitting miles apart. Then it quickly changed. I was lying on the couch with my knees up. You came across and lay down beside me and put your head on my shoulder as if for comfort and told me that things were bad for you. You didn't take tranquilizers because you didn't believe in them, but you add something to your diet (possibly a vitamin) that keeps you going.

"Then the scene opened up and we were in public. I was embarrassed to be seen with you like that and felt especially uneasy in front of a number of women who might have been your other patients. I got up and looked rather frantically in my handbag, but I couldn't find what I wanted. The contents were in chaos. I was very afraid."

It was clear to us both that the distance between us at the beginning of the dream referred to Petra's compulsive need to move her chair back, if only an inch or two, at the beginning of every session. (I had felt that this compulsion was in part a fear of being seduced by me and in part a fear of her own seductive effect on me.) Her main association was to her father, whose addiction was not to tranquilizers but to alcohol. He would sometimes return home the worse for drink and come upstairs and lie on the bed beside her, looking for affection and comfort. She was terrified by his physical presence, his seductive flamboyance, and his clear need. Although there was no genital touching, Petra realized with a mixture of terror and gratification that boundaries were being overstepped, that she was replacing her mother, and that there was a danger of an even greater sexual involvement. One thing that the dream identifies is the confusion between Petra's sexual, childlike, and maternal impulses toward her father. These distinctions also involve, among other things, the question of the patient's protective feelings toward the therapist. It was quite clear to me that Petra was deeply torn between her wish to seduce me and her maternal protectiveness toward me, which included a desire to spare me an intimacy that could harm me. But maternal strivings can, of course, be themselves a source of attraction. How much does a therapist, looking after his patients all day, crave at moments to be looked after by them?

After a session in which I had once again pointed out her extreme reluctance to speak of her feelings toward me, Petra had the following dream:

"A little girl was surrounded by a group of uncouth, sexually threatening men. I was horrified and moved in to protect her, saying, 'Can't you see she's too young for this? Go and find someone your own size.' Although she was a little girl, she was also a woman."

The dream depicts how Petra feels toward all men. It was precipitated, she realized, by comments of mine in the previous session, which she found threatening. "I don't know what there is to talk about," she said. "I wish you'd leave me alone. I don't want to think about it. I feel like running away." She appeared to experience my words themselves as threatening gestures, and I felt like a sexual monster. It was a moment when I felt considerable empathy with her previous therapist.

In the conversation that followed, she asserted that it was impossible to think of any relationship with me because she was only a child. "You should have a relationship with a proper grown woman," she said. It became progressively clearer that she was not talking to me but to a father who asked more of her than should be asked of a child and should have confined his sexual attentions to a grown-up woman.

But there is a further twist to this predicament, for, as is traditionally acknowledged, a childlike innocence and helplessness can be very seductive. There was, as I've suggested, something about Petra's vulnerability that was enormously appealing. She was a damsel in distress, and I (as, from her accounts, had several men before me) had strong rescue urges toward her. It may well be that part of her father's attraction to her lay in the fact that she was, unlike his powerful and responsible wife, a vulnerable child.

The source of Petra's anguish was, however, not confined to her involvement with her father. Behind him was the mother whom she could not hope to seduce or even please and to whom she must submit. Compared to the children who had come before her, she felt herself to be a great disappointment to her mother and despairingly withdrew from her in an attempt to escape incorporation and loss of identity. This is, I think, depicted in a fantasy in which she entered her own "attractive" house and discovered an inner room unknown to her. The room was dark, bare, and bleak with a bed in the corner. In the bed was a small child lying down, curled up, and facing the wall. It was pointless to try to communicate with this child. "It's very sad," she said. On another occasion she told me that the alternative to letting herself be molded by her mother would have been "to be left to die on the rocks—for I have no self."

The relationship with her father had led Petra to experience her sexuality as powerful and valued yet a source of tremendous risk. She compulsively needed to repeat this risk partly from the wish to gratify a deep and forbidden longing and partly in the hope that the father figure would be able to withstand her persuasiveness. Her previous therapy had, I fear, relived the encounters with her father to a degree that incapacitated her further rather than healed the trauma. The difficulty for any therapist in finding the most useful therapeutic stance to take toward Petra was in negotiating the narrow line between revealing fondness and acting in a seductive way and, conversely, in acknowledging her own genuine warmth yet recognizing that she was capable of seductive power.

Later on in the therapy, when I felt that we had negotiated these difficulties sufficiently well, I showed this account to the patient. Petra thought it a reasonably true description of her therapy but pointed out that in focusing on the question of seduction, I had presented a rather one-sided view of her and had done injustice to the genuine aspects of the relationships both with me and her previous therapist.

THE PSYCHOTHERAPIST'S DILEMMA

The question of the therapist's response to a patient's loving and sexual feelings was addressed with characteristic courage and honesty in a paper by Searles, "Oedipal Love in the Counter-transference," in which he criticized the current belief that passionate feelings in the therapist are a consequence of an unsatisfactory training analysis and are a source of potential harm to the patient. Searles (1965) maintains that such feelings validate the patient's sense of sexual worth in the same way that a parent's erotic fantasies about his child may promote a developing sexual identity. Although he advises caution in admitting such responses in therapy, he affirms that he had become

> less constrained to conceal these from the patient, and increasingly convinced that they augur well rather than ill for the outcome of our relationship, and that the patient's self-esteem benefits greatly from his sensing that he (or she) is capable of arousing such responses in the therapist. [p. 291]

He continues:

> All my experience with both neurotic and psychotic patients has indicated to me that, in every individual instance, in so far as the

oedipal phase was entered into in the course of their past development, it led to ego impairment rather than ego growth primarily because the beloved parent had to repress his or her reciprocal desire for the child, *chiefly through the mechanism of unconscious denial of the child's importance to the parent.* More often than not, in these instances, I find indications that the parent would unwittingly act out his or her repressed desires in the form of unduly seductive behaviour towards the child; but then, whenever the parent came close to the recognition of such desires within himself, he would unpredictably start reacting to the child as being unlovable, undesirable. [p. 303]

Searles writes with a passion that, although leading at times to overstatement, enables him to break through rigid formulae. We are left, however, with the familiar dilemma that the balance between openness and reticence often rests on a knife edge, and only our intuitive grasp of the patient's capacity to respond to a forthright approach will see us through. If we are too warm, he will either shrink away in fear or become enthralled by an imagined richness that cannot be matched in ordinary life.

Finally there is the question, "If therapist and patient fall in love with each other, and fail to restrain their feelings within the ordinary pursuit of accepted therapeutic measures, is the outcome necessarily catastrophic?" It would appear that there are cases, probably in the great minority, when this is not so. First, the two may dissolve the therapy and live happily together ever after. The letter of the law may have been disobeyed but its spirit is maintained. Second, even when a love affair takes place but ends in tears, it may be that more good may have been done than harm. A possible case in point is the notorious affair between Jung and Sabina Spielrein. Writing about Carotenuto's book on the subject, Bettelheim (1992) is severe in his criticism of Jung:

The difficulty in taking a balanced view of this matter is that there is no area where the dividing line between the life-enhancing forces of love, creativity, and passion and the necessary curtailment of these forces in certain circumstances is more indistinct. We can go astray by an irresponsible denial of the hazards and potential destructiveness of passionate love in therapy, but we may also make a total and even vicious condemnation of those who have taken the risk of breaking the taboo, and refuse to admit that the outcome is not universally harmful.

Carotenuto takes great pains to convince the reader that J
relation to Spielrein remained platonic; however, the docum
strongly suggest that this was not so. Obviously a psychoan
should not have sexual relations with his patient. Unfortun;
it has happened from time to time, with uniformly bad result
both patient and therapist. Some seventy years later, it
relatively little interest whether or not the great love Jung
Spielrein certainly felt for each other was sexually consumma
What seems much more important is whether the analyst
haved toward his patient-lover with respect and human decei
or whether he was concerned only for his public reputation,
not at all for the psychological vulnerability of his patient w
because he was her therapist, had no defences against him.
evidence is only too clear that Jung behaved toward Spielrei
a scandalous manner. [p. 62]

Yet he goes on to say:

Whatever may be one's judgement of Jung's behaviour tow;
Spielrein, probably his first psychoanalytic patient, one must r
disregard its most important consequence: he cured her from t
disturbance for which she had been entrusted to his care.
retrospect we ought to ask ourselves: what convincing eviden
do we have that the same result would have been achieved if Jur
had behaved toward her in the way we must expect a consciei
tious therapist to behave toward the patient? However questioi
able Jung's behaviour was from a moral point of view—howeve
unorthodox, even disreputable, it may have been—somehow
met the prime obligation of the therapist toward his patient: t
cure her. True, Spielrein paid a very high price in unhappiness
confusion and disillusion for the particular way in which she go
cured, but then this is often true for mental patients who are a
sick as she was. [p. 79]

Chapter Eleven

Responsibility

How can two walk together, except that they be agreed?
—Book of Amos

In health we take appropriate responsibility for our actions. Although this would appear to be a simple and straightforward way of behaving, it is one that we find extremely difficult in practice and a task that undermines and torments many of those who seek therapy. The sense of responsibility can be so crippling that the patient avoids it at enormous cost, expends an inordinate amount of energy in carrying out its demands, or is crushed by it to the point of paralysis. Guilt is the state of mind that occurs when we believe that we have failed in our responsibilities. This sense of failure may consist of justified remorse for an unworthy act or the consequence of an irrational and largely unconscious condemnation by the superego, that is to say, a conditioned response to remembered parental commands, to childhood expectation of parental retribution for fantasies thought to be wicked, or to an unmanageable hate that turns on the self in a destructive moral harangue. Much has been written about the distinction between guilt and shame. Shame, it would seem, is a word that best applies to a feeling of inadequacy, whether moral or otherwise, and is characteristically felt when an act unwittingly reveals something about oneself that is thought to be, at best, unadmirable, and at worst, despicable. Although a sense of shame makes a frequent appearance in the consulting room, the concept comes a very poor second to guilt in theoretical formulations.

The question of responsibility has been placed at the center of the stage by the existentialist psychotherapists who have made a cogent criticism of Freud's determinism, based on the thesis that natural science is an entirely inappropriate model for psychology since the essence of being human is to have choice. Given that this is the belief that we live by in our daily lives, it is a convincing attitude to take. One feature of their thinking is that we are responsible not only for others but for what we make of ourselves.

In an engaging and wise book, L. Farber (1976) suggests that anxiety is a consequence of willing what cannot be willed:

> I can will knowledge, but not wisdom; going to bed, but not sleeping; eating, but not hunger; meekness, but not humility; scrupulosity, but not virtue; self-assertion or bravado, but not courage; lust, but not love; commiseration, but not sympathy; congratulations, but not admiration; religiosity, but not faith; reading, but not understanding. I would emphasize that the consequence of willing what cannot be willed is that we fall into the distress we call anxiety. And since anxiety, too, opposes such willing, should we, in our anxiety about anxiety, now try to will away that anxiety, our fate is still more anxiety. Within this impasse, meaning, reason, imagination, discrimination fail, so that the will is deprived of its supporting and tempering faculties. [p. 7]

We live in a society, Farber believes, in which, having discounted the will of God we have, following Nietzsche, exaggerated the extent of our own powers to will and lost our capacity to experience mystery and to put ourselves in the hands of a fate that is beyond us. I believe this to be profoundly true.

And it would follow that we tend to have an exaggerated idea of the areas for which we can realistically be responsible.

RESPONSIBILITY BETWEEN THERAPIST AND PATIENT

If the therapist is to help his patient toward a more manageable sense of responsibility, he needs to have, above all, a realistic approach to his own powers and their limits, particularly in relation to his work. If the patient is left too much to her own devices, or if the therapist overestimates his own responsibility for the patient's life, little good will come from the endeavor. The therapist's attitude to this matter will not only mold the interpretations he makes (whether, for example, he focuses on the patient's own responsibility for his psychopathology or on the traumatic conditions that made health beyond his capacity to achieve) but dictate the degree to which, in practice, he helps the patient to find a balanced way of taking responsibility for herself in the consulting room. What then, we might ask, constitutes such a view?

Let us imagine two people in a room talking. We know nothing about them or why they are there. Have they any moral responsibility to each other?

In the broadest terms, in most people's ethical philosophy, they do: they should help rather than harm each other. To take an extreme example, if one of them takes seriously ill, we would expect the other to come to her aid. Put positively, the responsibility of each of the two people is to provide a reasonably life-enhancing environment for the other. It ought to be not too invasive or too rejecting, therefore, an acceptable boundary should be established. In any particular situation, there will be special factors affecting this balance. How does this apply in psychotherapy?

It would appear at first sight that there is complete imbalance in psychotherapy. One person is responsible for the other. Insofar as therapy follows the medical model, this is certainly how it would seem to be. The doctor gives pills; the patient takes them and dies; the doctor is responsible. The doctor gives pills; the patient flushes them down the toilet and dies; the patient is responsible. Thus, the responsibility of the patient is merely to do, without question, what the doctor orders. She is, to an extent, responsible for her own life, but only within this formula. How well does psychotherapy fit this conception? In orthodox psychoanalysis, the patient is asked to lie on the couch and to freely associate—to speak rather than to act—and usually obeys this request. The analyst, then, interprets. The patient's responsibility is to take the "medicine" to try to benefit from the analyst's recreated narrative of her life. In other words, the analyst knows how things should be done in the consulting room. The salient features of the interaction are unknown to the patient, not only because of her ignorance of the theory and technique but because they are buried in her unconscious. She has no control over them and no responsibility for them. There is, however, another side to the analyst's expectations, for he believes that the patient does in fact need to have responsibility—to possess therapeutic drive—and, indeed, regards the acquisition of self-responsibility as one of the aims, if not the main aim, of therapy.

Those who come for help are, to an extent, passive; they have lost their autonomy. The abrogation of responsibility that is most striking is that which is often termed *hysterical*. A patient who is acting under the force of this attitude controls others by accentuating her own weak position. She dramatizes her plight but never nakedly exposes her vulnerability or places herself in another's power. To free such a person from a passive role in the performance of which she has become adept and which preserves her from the terror of closeness is an extraordinarily difficult task. The therapist must avoid being seduced into taking more responsibility for the patient's life yet can hardly stand back calmly observing the self-destruction as if it wasn't his business.

No one has spelled out the need to confront the patient with his passivity more clearly than Roy Schafer (1976), who maintains that the analyst steadily encourages activity in the patient as opposed to the acceptance of herself as a victim of circumstance, and attempts to guide her away from such disclaimers as, for example, "The thought of revenge suggested itself," or "I can't help it; it's my unconscious."

We are faced, therefore, with a paradox. At the same time as we encourage responsibility in the patient, we also permit her to be irresponsible. We say, as it were: "Let rip. I want all your infantile hate and love to emerge without any holding back. Attack me, reject me, crave for me—anything you like. You don't have to feel any responsibility for what happens to me." By virtue of this idea, the patient is allowed to do almost anything short of killing the therapist. She can shout, insult, scream, kick, walk out, seduce, or break vases, and the therapist goes on trying to understand it all.

How can one solve this paradox? In practice, I think it is a matter of intuition. We have to gauge the degree to which, at any moment, the patient should and could take responsibility for her actions—to assess the baby and the adult in her. To get this right is one of the hardest arts of psychotherapy. However, faulty theory or technique can get in our way. If our aim is to encourage responsibility in the patient, then it would seem to be more appropriate to do so from the beginning and to provide a set-up that is as far removed from the medical model as we can manage. There are two ways in which this can be done.

First, what happens between patient and therapist could be made as negotiable as possible. Thus, the patient may lie on the couch, sit in the chair, sit on the floor, sit in the psychotherapist's chair, bring her husband or her dog, have her session in a boat on the river, or ask for the therapist's life story—provided that these options are personally acceptable to the therapist. This does not mean that the therapist should accommodate those of the patient's wishes that he regards as defensive measures. He is even entitled, after reflection, to be quite strict, to say, "I can help you only if you do X, Y, or Z," but such edicts can be dangerous and lead to overcontrol and exploitation. It would seem, in general, that an insistence by the therapist on a relationship that departs from ordinary humane and virtuous behavior is to be regarded with suspicion. One thing that the therapist can never negotiate is the fact that he remains the therapist, and the patient remains the patient. Otherwise therapy has ended. In looking at the matter in this way, we are shifting the emphasis onto the positive rather than the negative. We do not deny the patient's helplessness, but we look for, and encourage, her sense of responsibility both to herself and to the therapist. Even the sickest of people retain some agency.

Second, we could encourage the patient to recognize her effect on the therapist, to realize that her words and actions are not falling on thin air but on a real person, who may be warmed or hurt by them. It is confusing to pretend otherwise, for how else is the patient to learn this reality? It would seem that, within the limits of protecting the patient from undue anxiety and hurt, and allowing for the value of tact, we should let her know that she affects us. Because of our therapeutic stance, we will not be at all likely, for example, to retaliate with anger as we would in ordinary life, but sometimes it is not *necessarily* inappropriate for the therapist to get angry, to shout, cry, hug, and even throw cold water over the patient. I believe that I have hurt my patients much more by withholding than by giving a manifestly emotional response.

Because the patient's inability to take responsibility for her effect on others is usually so central to her psychopathology, it is important that she be given as much opportunity as possible to understand the impression that the patient and her therapist have on each other and to work out a concept of joint responsibility. To this end, the therapist needs to spell out as far as possible his experience and judgment of the patient's impact; disclose his own aims, wishes, and fantasies in regard to the patient; and recognize that by simply being the sort of person he is and holding the beliefs that he does he will unwittingly influence the other (Lomas 1987).

THE RESTRAINT OF THE THERAPIST

In what sense does the therapist's responsibility differ from that of the patient? The obvious one is that whatever else might be going on, the therapist is committed to trying to heal the patient. He is required to bring his experience and his position as observer in order to reflect in ways not possible for the patient. He needs to be able to have hope and to see continuity where she cannot. To do this, he has to put many of his own needs in the background in order to listen. This applies not only to intrusive thoughts from his own life, which might distract him, but to some of the responses evoked by the patient. He must contain his tendency to moan, boast, retaliate and chat aimlessly, and so on. The enormous difficulty of maintaining this stance is accentuated by the need to look for clues to the patient's unconscious. The consequence of attempting this Herculean task is that the profession has understandably tended to emphasize restraint, as is enshrined in Freud's papers on technique, in which he states that the analyst must appear impenetrable to the patient and must cultivate the attitude of a surgeon. There is, however, a potential misapprehension in this view. If it is the case (as I have suggested earlier) that in order to understand the patient and to provide a healing relationship the therapist needs to form as intimate a relationship with her as circumstances permit, then restraint can be counterproductive. To break through her withdrawal and mistrust, the therapist may need to show his passion, risk revealing vulnerability, and risk hurt and perhaps humiliation. This, I think, is the message of Ferenczi. It also means, as I suggested in the previous chapter, taking the risk that we may seduce the patient into loving us and then be unable to handle her feelings or our own. Our narcissism can lead us to err in either direction, either to take the restrained, cynical, shrewd, worldly line "I won't be manipulated or exploited by anybody. This is just hysteria and needs to be dealt with firmly" or "I risk more, am more loving, will put myself out more than my unfeeling colleagues."

A sense of responsibility is, like perception or judgment, an elemental ingredient of any authentic relationship. It need not, perhaps cannot, be spelled out and prescribed. To do so would be to make it into a technique rather than a human quality. It accompanies love, but it can operate at times when love is absent, when we have, for whatever reason, committed ourselves to a person or a cause. Inauthentic responsibility, on the other hand, can derive from a urge to acquire power or status by controlling the other through various maneuvers, for instance, presenting oneself as morally superior and therefore in possession of the greater truth. It can also originate in a fear of being thought irresponsible, or it could be the consequence of an unconscious need to contradict one's hate. Thus, moral earnestness may serve as a vehicle for many different and devious aims. In the therapist, an inauthentic sense of responsibility can lead to pompousness, coercion, or the unnecessary reserve characteristic of the respectable and adult professional who is controlling, at the expense of risk, spontaneity, fun and those ordinary ways of relating that are vital to human growth.

THE ETHICAL CODE

Finally, there is the matter of an ethical code. Should psychotherapists' behavior, both professional and private, be controlled by a code of practice laid down by the state or their own organizations? The belief that they should is one of the reasons— perhaps the chief reason—behind the present drive toward the establishment of a register of psychotherapists. Indeed, it has sometimes been said that given the well-nigh impossibility of forming a professional register on the basis of a unified theory of psychotherapy, the only meaningful code of practice would be based on ethics. At the time of writing, therapeutic training organizations in Britain are formulating codes of ethics in order to conform to the demands of the proposed register of practitioners. How justified and how useful is this endeavor? It is, I believe, a question of where the focus lies.

If we were to make a radical attempt to reduce crime, to what area should we give our main attention? Should we build bigger prisons, increase the number of police, and introduce stiffer penalties? Or should we try to create conditions in which a life without crime appears more desirable, more accessible, and morally acceptable? Those who have a preference for the latter approach (as I do myself) may consider that the course of action most likely to produce therapists who behave well toward their patients is to select prospective students who are sincerely concerned for the predicament of others and to encourage such an attitude in their training. The therapist who, as an autonomous human being, puts his patient's interests at the center of his work, is the least likely to behave in ways that are commonly considered unethical.

Chapter Twelve

Is Psychotherapy Real?

Irony can afford the only possible victory in the face of defeat, a "moral victory" in the line of Pascal's saying—that man is only a reed, the weakest thing in nature, but he is a thinking reed. The universe, or accident, or disease, may get the better of him, but whereas he knows this, the universe, the accident, the disease, know nothing of it. The snag is that a disposition towards irony, though it may not invite defeat, accepts it too readily.

—D. J. Enright

A man whom I had been seeing for a year came in for his session and immediately asked: "Why do you put your arms behind your head? Is it to convey that you are relaxed, or cool, or whatever?"

He said this in the manner of an interested observer of life, which prompted me to reply: "You speak generally and not personally, not specifically. Not: 'It matters to me what Peter's attitude is. Is he interested? Is he really at ease with me? What is he really thinking?' You don't follow it up. You avoid the reality of your relationships."

"But this isn't a real relationship! You can't compare this to the outer world. It's not social life! It's not business!"

"What's the difference? Why is this any less real than other areas of your life?"

At this point he became quite unusually upset. "You're making me angry. I feel panic. I feel like walking out."

"That's because I've managed to get you to consider that this relationship is a real one."

This interchange led to a painful discussion of his ways of escaping from the potential hurt and disappointment should he give himself to someone and be rejected. His ready assumption that the therapeutic encounter was so different from ordinary life that one didn't have to take it quite seriously played into his defenses. I am aware that in claiming that our relationship is a real one I ignored the fact that we unconsciously played games with each other (was I really "relaxed" or, as he suggested, inauthentically conveying a relaxation that I didn't have?), but this does not distinguish it from other areas of living.

I will give another example.

Richard's basic problem was that he did not quite connect with his life. He functioned very successfully, but his heart was not in it; it was the same in therapy, which, given the understanding he had gained about his motives and defenses, should have been more successful than it was. When I confronted him with this fact, he readily agreed, remaining characteristically poised about the matter. I then said that if the therapy did not address this central issue, perhaps we should stop. Richard became annoyed and discouraged. "Why are you angry?" I asked. "I wouldn't mind," he said, "if you were just trying to provoke a response, but I know you mean it. I don't like people to take me seriously."

A little later on we had the following exchange. I suggested that he was very careful with me.

"Like, for instance, I won't lie on the couch?"

"Yes. But perhaps, even more, you never make any move. You sit in the chair in the same position all the time. You wouldn't dream of, say, standing up."

"I would feel awkward."

"I think it's your way of fitting in with a role. You try to disappear into the role, to make yourself invisible."

"Yes. I would freeze if it were just me."

"Don't you need to take the risk?"

"Not on my own. There's no one to be with me."

"What about here?"

"Here it's not the same. It wouldn't count anyway. You don't mind what I say. You put up with me."

"Doesn't "here" connect with the outer world?"

"No, it's like learning Chinese and not going to China."

"Isn't it that you are afraid to take the risk that would lead us to a different, more real, kind of relationship."

"That frightens me."

It was clear that for Richard, the therapy, although quite rigorous in some ways, was a kind of game. It was as though he had been telling me jokes, and I had suddenly, unfairly, taken him at his word.

Another conversation with him was as follows:

Richard said, "You sometimes ask me why I'm not curious about you. I don't see why I should be. I could ask, for instance, whether you like Mozart or Wagner. But so what? Anyway, psychotherapy shouldn't be like that. Psychotherapy isn't friendship. I want to keep you as someone of my imagination."

"Why?"

"We all need dreams in life. And I just want you to try and fix things. Like getting my car fixed."

"So you're trying to diminish my importance?"

"Yes. If you died tonight I'd have to get another therapist. It would be inconvenient. But if you were personally important that wouldn't be possible."

It was clear that behind Richard's wish to avoid thinking of me as a real person who might take him seriously, jolt him into life, and impinge on his emotions he had to keep me as a fantasy figure and see the therapy as a kind of performance outside of life. In both the cases that I've quoted, the nature of the therapeutic set-up enabled the patient to avoid disturbing emotions, which would have occurred had the encounter been seen as a part of real life.

THE PRESENTATION OF REALITY IN THE CONSULTING ROOM

I should at this point say something about the concept "real," which has a checkered history and still eludes a consensus about its meaning. The ideal, universal realities of Plato were of a very different nature from the stone kicked by Dr. Johnson.

In more recent years, philosophers have emphasized the degree to which we construct our realities: a stone is not simply a stone but the meaning it has for us as one item in a complex interpretation of life. That we construct meanings in this sense is indisputable. But philosophy and linguistics have, in recent years, led us so far down this path that the reality of an actual world has all but vanished. The only answer to this is, I believe, akin to that of Pascal, who told us to live as though God existed, that is, to live by faith. In our daily lives, we do in fact live by means of our faith that reality exists, and have no other way of living.

In the context of psychotherapy, we need to ask ourselves what we mean by the term *real* when speaking of human relationships and to explore the extent and manner in which the psychotherapeutic set-up promotes or prevents the emergence of that which is real. The nearest I can get to what we mean by the term as we use it in ordinary life is to say that a real relationship is one in which two people engage each other with the minimum of pretense about what is happening between them and in which the relationship itself is of paramount significance. This places it in opposition to engagements that are trivial, superficial, inauthentic, insincere, manipulative, or in which the two people are quite explicitly pretending that something is happening which is not, as, for example, when Julius Caesar gets a knife in his back on the stage.

In psychotherapy, the patient has to make this kind of assessment: to consider how real, in the sense I am using the word, is the encounter. Let us begin our enquiry by looking at the scene as it might present itself to the eyes of a patient.

A person enters a psychotherapist's office. It may have an impressively esoteric and ritualistic atmosphere: the couch, the books, the Oriental rug, the picture of Freud on the wall, the restrained greeting. Alternatively, it could be informal, commonplace, and unspectacular, with the therapist giving a friendly "Hello!" The distinction between these two styles is a highly significant one and will color the subsequent drama, but in either case the set-up is a unique one. It is not like any other relationship in life. The therapist presents herself as someone who has, for whatever reason, the authority to save others, to heal the wounds of life; there is an agreement that many of the conventions of daily exchanges do not apply; the patient has permission to be silent, to cry, to vilify the therapist, to speak obscenely, to admit suicidal or homicidal impulses, and so on, and will not be shown the door or turned over to the police.

What is one to think of such a place? It is an oasis, a haven from the rigors of living. "Who is this person," the patient may ask, "who responds in this extraordinarily unselfish way and who appears to know about people? Is he pretending to tolerate me? He must be a saint to put up with all this garbage." Or possibly: "He places me in the category of a nonperson, a case, an example of a disease process so that what I say and do does not touch him in the usual way and need not be taken seriously."

If I think of the ways in which patients have a distorted perception of me, they tend to fall into these two patterns.

Either they idealize me or, with sadness and perhaps bitterness, they assume that they have little meaning to me beyond that of a person to whom I am bound by a contract to address in certain technical ways. These two perceptions may, of course, be present at the same time, held together by spurious thinking.

The patient's attitude can, usually with justification, be explained in terms of transference or various defense mechanisms, but such explanations may easily obscure the fact that he is being placed in a situation that stands in striking contrast to his experience of intimacy in ordinary life. How does he know whether the therapist's attitude is a mask? The therapist is giving two messages that seem to be in opposition to each other. On the one hand, she shows care and concern for the patient, listening with attention, interest, and empathy to his deepest anguish and intimate revelations in the way that might be expected only from a loving relative or friend. Yet on the other hand, she claims her fee, turns out her client at the end of fifty minutes, and refuses to have any social contact with him. This confusing picture derives in part from the fact that professionalism and intimacy are uneasy bedfellows.

The discrepancy between what appears to be a possibility and what cannot be fulfilled is enacted in a particularly sharp and tantalizing way but is not, however, a unique situation. In many areas of life—in friendship, in teaching, in parenting, in marriage—there are limitations on intimacy, boundaries that cannot be crossed or can be negotiated only with great risk. Yet we do not usually designate these areas as unreal, as entirely remote from the rest of life. There is, however, another reason why psychotherapy may be regarded as unreal: the peculiar type of dialogue encouraged by the psychoanalytic method.

Freud, as we know, developed the technique of free association as a means of unveiling the unconscious. Instead of talking, as in ordinary life, in a way designed to have a direct effect on the other person, the patient was asked to speak without reference to the impact of his words on the analyst, reporting whatever came into his mind, as if he were speaking into thin air. Relieved from the expectation of talking in conventional, coherent, sane, and polite terms, he became aware of thoughts that would otherwise be suppressed. Freud observed that the mere release from conventional dialogue did not give immediate access to what was hidden, because the patient himself was too afraid of self-knowledge to allow this to happen easily. The analyst, therefore, must try to understand the reasons for this fear, and in order to accomplish this task, he should detach himself from the patient's conscious assertions and look behind them to discover what was being concealed.

The degree to which the analyst regards his patient's words as unrealistic, as not having direct relevance to actual living, has been starkly described by Forrester (1990), who in writing about Freud's rule of technique asserts that "an implicit function of that rule is that no action shall be taken on the basis of what is said"; the analyst's message is, "Say whatever comes into your head, but you cannot expect me to place any faith in what you say, or take anything you say at face value" (p. 44).

This rule is not something that we can dismiss easily. By its means, Freud unveiled facts about human beings that have changed our social and cultural life and that are still regarded by most psychotherapists as of the utmost importance to their understanding of sickness and healing. Moreover, it could be said that what Freud unveiled was more real, more authentic, than the conscious discourse of the patient. But it is not as simple as that.

To say that our ordinary, everyday speech often falls lamentably short of the truth—that we lie, are hypocritical, and that many of our motives and fantasies are hidden from us—is, of course, undeniable. But to build a theory of living based on

this skeptical and cynical vision—to assert that our consciousness is but a cloak to conceal the truth—is another matter. Freud
went some way in this direction, and it has been taken considerably further by Lacan and the deconstructionists. Moreover,
neither Freud nor Lacan nor you nor I believe that this is the
case, for we do not act on it.

Lacan (1988) was well aware of the paradox involved in
psychoanalytic technique—the fact that in order to reach reality
we ask the patient to dispense with any attempt to address us in
a realistic way:

> The analytic method, if it aims at attaining full speech, starts off
> on a path leading in the diametrically opposed direction, in so far
> as it instructs the subject to delineate a speech as devoid as
> possible of any assumption of responsibility and that it even frees
> him from any expectation of authenticity. It calls on him to say
> everything that comes into his head. It is through these very
> means that it facilitates, that is the least one can say, his return
> on to the path which, in speech, is below the level of recognition.
> [p. 108]

Such deviousness does not bother Lacan because of his
contempt for any conscious search for truth; but there are
problems in this method for those of us who have survived the
twentieth century's assault on the possibility of authentic interaction. I have given two illustrations to indicate the danger of
encouraging the patient to think of therapy as something unreal
and quite separate from the kind of relationships he experiences
in the rest of his life—a relationship in which his responsibility to
the other is minimal. Let me approach the matter by reference to
the work of Schafer (1976).

Schafer argues that in ordinary life we tend to avoid full
responsibility for our actions by using a phraseology designed to
disclaim them. Examples of such disclaimers are:

"The impulse seized me."

"My conscience torments me."

"One part of me says 'Yes' and another part says 'No.' "

In place of such forms of speech, Schafer suggests that we use what he refers to as "action language," that we more readily attribute responsibility to ourselves and replace circumlocutions by such statements as "I will," "I won't," "I decided," and so forth.

The fundamental rule of psychoanalysis "Say everything that comes into your mind" is, in Schafer's view, an invitation to disclaim responsibility and a seduction into passivity:

> According to the action model, the statement of the fundamental rule should convey the sense of the following ideas: "I shall expect you to talk to me each time you come. As you talk, you will notice that you refrain from saying certain things. You may do so because you want to avoid being trivial, irrelevant, embarrassed, tactless, or otherwise disruptive. It is essential to our work that you do this as little as possible. I urge you to tell me of those instances of selection or omission no matter what their content may be". Similarly, rather than "What comes to mind?", the kind of question that is conceptually and technically exact according to the action model is, "What do you think of in this connection?" or "What do you now connect with that?" or "If you think of this, what do you think of next?" Which is to say that thoughts come and go only as we think them or stop thinking them, or in other words, that thinking is a kind of action engaged in by persons. We are responsible for all our thoughts, including, as Freud pointed out, our dreams. Yet both the fundamental rule as usually formulated and the question "What comes to mind?" imply the negation of this proposition, the very proposition on which interpretation is based. [Schafer 1976, p. 147]

In other words, Freud's attempt to increase the patient's capacity for taking responsibility for himself is subverted by the very form in which he couched his enquiry. This withdrawal from action can and does, I believe, go even further. The conventional psychoanalytic dialogue encourages the patient to think, "It is not me saying it; it is not you hearing it. The whole thing is a pretense. It is not real." It could be argued that a technique designed to obstruct someone's conscious perception and sense of immediate reality in order to gain access to the unconscious can be so crucial to success that this consideration overrides any other. It is certainly true that in a critical or apparently hopeless situation one may resort to almost any measure. But it is a different matter to use, as a matter of principle and on all patients, a technique that deprives them of experiences that are central to the development of reality-sense and of privileges accorded to human beings in a democratic society (for example, the ability to use their unimpaired judgment). At the least, one has to weigh whatever possible gains may accrue from such a measure against the loss of autonomy that it involves. I do not think that psychoanalysis has ever quite recognized what a bizarre and potentially dangerous thing it is to act as though the patient's words have no personal impact.

FRAMES OF REFERENCE

In order to get a balanced view of this problem, it is, I believe, necessary to recognize the fact that fantasy, play, free association, and similarly ungrounded ways of behaving are safe only *within* the context of a relationship that is considered a real one. One might legitimately say in the course of a conversation in daily life, "I think I want to run away from everything and become a hermit. But don't take me seriously. I don't mean I'm really going to do it"; and there is no confusion. Similarly, the patient in therapy may say, "I have a fantasy that I want to destroy your genitals," and there is no confusion. But it needs to be stated that therapist and patient do, in fact, have a real relationship in which such fantasies have an impact and meaning, and that if this basic realistic assessment of the situation is lost, things will go wrong. I will give an example.

A therapist told his patient that he was so worried about him that he would have to take a course of action that involved a betrayal of confidentiality. This was unacceptable to the patient, who went home and wrote a letter saying that, with regret, he was stopping therapy and could he have the bill. The therapist replied that his letter was to be seen as a negative transference that needed further analysis. This kind of interchange occurred several times, and the patient began to feel that he was quite unable to make the therapist aware that he really meant what he said, that is, that whether or not the therapist had a valid point, he, the patient, had the right to leave and had made his decision. In this case the patient, because he had made a firm decision, was in no danger; but when this kind of happening occurs while dependency is great, the outcome could be more harmful.

For this reason, the therapist is wise to be very cautious about merely interpreting the words of a patient who appears to mean what he says. This has, of course, to be balanced by those cases, which occur both in ordinary life and in therapy, when someone is taunting or testing out and wishes his pretense to be seen through. The important factor is to be able to distinguish between "I mean it" and "Don't take me seriously" whatever the situation in which the statement occurs. It is not enough to assume that during the therapeutic fifty minutes nothing is to be taken seriously and afterwards the opposite applies, for every therapist realizes that there is no clear distinction. What is necessary is for a person to know that his listener will make a sensitive assessment of the mode in which a statement is made and will be flexible enough to respond to an urgent request that is meant seriously. When two people are wrestling in play, it is imperative for one of them to be able to say, "You're hurting me. Stop," and be listened to.

What does this line of thought imply in practice? One way of looking at the question is to do so in terms of what Goffman (1975) refers to as a *frame of reference*. The primary frame of reference in psychotherapy, it would seem, should be based on the fact that, in simple terms and in all seriousness, one person is trying to help another. It is not a game, a play, a drama; it is real. Both parties are involved; either or both may be hurt. Within the context of this primary frame of reference, certain things may happen that temporarily shift the frame. As in ordinary life, there may be jokes and play; and, particularly in psychotherapy, there may be indulgence in fantasy. While these events are going on, it will be understood that not everything is to be taken literally. (In the context of this discussion, I am making a clear distinction between seriousness and play, which, I recognize, cannot always be made.) Things go wrong when the primary frame of reference is lost, when, for example, there is a pretense that the relationship is one of play, that the hurtful or loving words of the patient do not matter and do not affect the therapist as a person in any way whatsoever.

The distortion that occurs when we do not take the fact of the therapeutic relationship seriously is one in which there is an alteration to the significance of the gestalt from the center to the periphery. Although the relationship between patient and therapist inevitably has overtones (products of memory, fantasy, and imagination), to give all our attention to the overtones will result in Hamlet without the prince. In order to preserve the center of things we must, I believe, not only take the patient's words and actions seriously but respond as a person seriously affected by them. If we do not do so, the patient's capacity to believe that he has a firm place in the world and can actively effect change will be discouraged. There is, moreover, a further danger. The therapist who puts fantasy at the center of therapy is in danger of ignoring not only the reality inside the consulting room but that of the outside world—the conflicts and burdens of the patient's existence in the present, especially the dynamics of the family or social network in which he lives.

Every priority carries its own limitations. If it is the case, as I suggest, that the real relationship should be the center of the therapeutic encounter, it is necessary to look at what might be lost when this is so. The crucial question to ask is, "To what extent is the therapeutic relationship inevitably based on illusion?" or, to put the case more strongly, "Should the therapist foster or create illusion?" If by staying with the actuality of the relationship we lose our capacity to interpret the patient's unconscious, we would have thrown away the gifts that Freud has given us. But I believe that we need not make such a sacrifice.

THE PSYCHOTHERAPIST AS ILLUSIONIST

That the evocation of the illusion of transference is the essence of psychoanalytic technique has been made explicit by John Klauber (1987) in his book *The Role of Illusion in the Psychoanalytic Cure*, but the dividing line between making room for illusions to appear and creating conditions that foster illusions and dictate the form in which they emerge is a narrow one. As I discussed earlier (Chapter 6), transference will appear without resort to special technique provided we do not squash it, and I would suggest that, for those of us who are aware of the phenomenon, the danger of overlooking transference is considerably less than that of distorting it by acting in rehearsed or inauthentic ways.

There is another reason why the therapist may wish to create illusion: the need to gain the patient's trust. This can be subsumed under the concept of transference, for, as Freud maintained, an idealized transference will give the patient the necessary wish and confidence to get better. This use of transference is, however, to be distinguished from that which depends on recognizing former patterns of behavior that have become inappropriate.

To what extent, we might ask, should the therapist woo her patients? Would they have the confidence to put themselves in her hands if they did not, at least at the beginning, have an exaggerated notion of her powers? The history of healing reveals a long-established conviction that it is necessary to seduce the patient into false beliefs (Ellenberger 1970).

In her book *Implicit Meanings*, Mary Douglas (1975) contrasts the views on healing rites of the anthropologists Levi-Strauss and Victor Turner. Levi-Strauss takes as his model the charismatic figure of the American Indian shaman, who dazzles by the skill of his conjuring and the force of his personality. In Levi-Strauss's own words: "Quesalid did not become a great shaman because he cured his patients: he cured his patients because he became a great shaman" (Levi-Strauss 1968, p. 180). The ritual is a private affair: "Doctor and patient might be alone (for all explanatory purposes) in an imagined universe constructed by the shaman specially for the seance" (p. 180).

Although Victor Turner's Ndemby shaman is also a conjuror who, in Douglas's words, "produces by sleight of hand objects from the sufferer's body," his style is more that of the psychiatric social worker who takes due note of social structure and encourages clients to conform to the moral norms of their culture. "To this end he gets them to dramatize their situation in an established ritual idiom. At the same time he skilfully manipulates their relationships" (Douglas 1975, p. 147).

What light does this throw on contemporary psychotherapy? The therapist works, like Quesalid, in a very intimate private world with her patient, undistracted by the noise and the intrusions of daily life. It is an admirable setting to facilitate any charisma that the practitioner might possess.

In a paper in which he discusses charisma, Hayley (1990) observes that psychoanalysts appear to turn a blind eye on their suggestive influence over patients. He maintains that analysts "add to their personal charisma by publishing books and papers and even holding high offices in our societies" and believes that the practice of keeping themselves anonymous from their patients is a further measure of their attempt to foster charisma. It would appear that although therapists neither use the gadgetry of the shaman nor isolate their patients in an enclosed setting quite as effectively as does the monastery or convent, they do have means at their disposal for exerting enormous suggestive pressure, among which is the prestige of the professional.

A ritual, like a conversation, is designed to influence. The ritualistic elements in psychotherapy, largely overlooked by practitioners, should surely nudge them to question the rational justifications that are currently made for their technique, although it does not necessarily follow that the rituals themselves are therefore invalid and disadvantageous. This would be the case only if they were meaningless and deadening, if they were used to convey a harmful or confusing message, or if they were performed in a way that was too coercive. Sadly, however, when we try to influence others—even if our aim is primarily a benign one—we seem irresistibly drawn to mystifying and devious methods.

It is very difficult to distinguish between a communication that is coercive and one that is not. As I write this book, I attempt to put my views in as effective a way as I can manage. Although I try to avoid lies or crude propagandist statements, I use whatever power of reasoning I possess, and I take note of current social values in seeking to persuade the reader of my views. And even had I the subtlety and integrity of the great artist, I would not be exempt from the charge of seducing the reader into faulty thinking. A distinction of this kind can never be precise but depends on our judgment in every situation. The delicate task of the psychotherapist is to encourage and to give hope where hope is realistic while respecting the patient's autonomy, and doing her best to avoid overpersuasion by means of her status and supposed wisdom. On the other hand, it would be foolish of her to make a show of all her failings and incompetences. The following is an example of the kind of situation in which this kind of judgment has to be made.

Betty told me, on arrival for her session, that there was a police speed trap in operation in a nearby road. Did I know? I answered that I did, and that I myself had recently been stopped by the police for speeding at the same place. "Did they give you a ticket?" she asked. I answered that I had exaggerated the medical importance of my journey and had not been charged. She was surprised and a little shocked that I would tell a white lie to get myself out of trouble. "You must think me a very proper person," I said. Betty agreed that she did. I commented that she took good care to maintain this illusion by avoiding opportunities to question me or get to know me because she was afraid of finding out my fallibility.

"Yes, I don't want to know about you. It's safer like that."

I reminded her, however, that she had had the fantasy that I was responsible for a recent murder that had occurred locally. I suggested that her apparent security was, to a degree, spurious, that she did not entirely trust me, and that this was the reason for her extremely cautious behavior in sessions with me.

The consequence of my revelation in this interchange was not, I believe, a simple disillusionment. I am not sure whether my response to Betty was helpful or not, but if it had any significant impact on her, it seems likely that this would be in the direction of helping her to see me as a whole, flawed person rather than a divided entity of saint and sinner. It did not appear that my admission diminished her trust in my capacity to help. And I believe that a gradual, piece-by-piece ability to challenge and undermine illusions would seem likely to help avoid the growth of a persistent and gross distortion unfavorable to the open and honest communication that engenders trust.

IMAGINATION

Finally, I wish to consider the place of imagination and play in therapy. The task of therapy can be seen as one of lifting a patient from a drab and limited experience of living, enlarging his horizons, and stimulating his imagination. The patient who is passive, depressed, rigid, and lost will be helped if the therapist can enable him to recapture his potential for growth and to visualize a world that is more receptive to his intentions than he had believed. Vision is the capacity to imagine a richer experience than the immediate one, a capacity that permits hope and risk, and, indeed, is an essential requirement of fruitful living.

Writing of imagination, Stuart Hampshire (1989) asserts:

> We have been deceived, both in our lives and in the criticism of art and literature, by a conventional and superficial picture of the self. The true and singular self of each individual is buried below the reach of introspection and of conscious attention. With effort and dedication it can be brought into the light of imagination, if and only if we probe into the original sources of

our more inexplicable and irrational feelings, however improbable and accidental the sources may seem. A deadening incrustation of conventional classifications of human concerns, and of human powers, prevents us from looking inwards and from recognising the un-named exaltations and depressions of our inner life for what they are the revelations of our real nature, concealed by our social role. Instead of trying to conform to generalised and established models of human distinction, of standardised intelligence and of approved tastes, we should strive to extract and to express the singular responses of our own sensibility and of our unique perceptions. We know the responses to be an authentic disclosure of our own true nature when they are associated with an emotional force which cannot be explained by any reasonable calculation. [p. 128]

This essentially respectful attitude toward the uniqueness of the other person would seem to be the one least likely to coerce or brainwash him into a path that is less a new way of being than a false alternative to his old one.

In the classical psychoanalytic view, the production of fantasy is essential to cure because it reveals what is wrong and what must be replaced; the pleasure principle must give way to the reality principle. Winnicott, Milner, Rycroft, and others have now shown that fantasy can be seen to have another, and equally profound, significance, that of a component of play and imagination directed toward reality and an essential element in growth.

In both imagination and illusion, the subject departs from his present sense of reality. In illusion, the departure involves a split with reality; it is a misperception of what is or what can be. We have lost our hold on the present reality and substitute another one. (Colloquially, illusion is usually taken to mean the misperception that things are better than is really the case. We see the world through rose-colored spectacles. The complementary word *disillusionment* also has this connotation: those in such a state realize, in dismay, that things are worse than they had thought.) If, however, the therapist wishes to encourage vision and promote change, may he not need, in wrenching the patient away from his narrow and apparently secure path, to create illusion, if only temporarily? May he not be obliged to be subtle and manipulative—a conjuror, in fact? Is it not true that imagination can be stimulated by art and artifice? I believe it can, but, as I suggested earlier, the degree to which we depart from reality is crucial. There is a parallel with sexuality. We may have all kinds of fantasies about the loved one, which enrich our bond, but if they are its mainstay, we are in trouble. Moreover, the term *illusion*, by which these authors describe what occurs in the intermediate, experimental stage of the search for reality, is, to my mind, used in a misleading way. On our journey through unknown territory, using whatever means we can in order to tread the right path, we will try various routes and look for helpful signs, and will inevitably make mistakes on the way. We need to be flexible enough to *risk* having illusions, but they are not valuable in themselves and are not necessarily to be encouraged.

In any situation in life, it is difficult to know the extent to which we are under the influence of illusion. An illusion may involve not only a denial or simple ignorance of some part of reality but the neglect of many potential perceptions while one focuses concentration upon one particular item. It is a matter of degree. To the extent that we cannot, emotionally or intellectually, give full reception to all aspects of reality, we are inevitably in a state of illusion. The patient who feels love for his therapist often knows little about her beyond what can be perceived in the unusual circumstances of the consulting room. But those aspects of the therapist that appear lovable and admirable may be quite genuinely there in the room at the time. And the fact that the patient may be reminded of rich experiences with a parent (which he actually had or merely dreamed of) does not mean he is deluded that the therapist is his parent. Although it remains true that the opportunities for illusion are even greater in therapy than in ordinary life, I would suggest that what puts the patient more in touch with his emotions is a real experience rather than an illusory one and is therapeutic if fantasies, when they occur, are soundly embedded in what is real in the relationship. It is, admittedly, not easy to make this distinction. In ordinary life, we have to try to assess the authenticity of our personal relationships – to make the often very difficult distinction between loving someone and being in love with their image – and it is no different and no less crucial in therapy.

Chapter Thirteen

Ordinariness

When a philosopher raises doubts about time or about mental states, that do not occur to the ordinary man, this is not because the philosopher has more insight than the ordinary man, but because, in a way, he has less; he is subject to temptations to misunderstand that do not occur to the non-philosopher.

—Ray Monk

In this chapter, I use the word *ordinary* in the customary dictionary sense of "unexceptional." We are all ordinary insofar as we have the qualities that make us human beings; we are neither gods nor apes. This fact does not, of course, stop us from being uniquely different from all others of our species and therefore unusual.

There are those who, by virtue of a particular feature (big ears, a loud voice) make them prominent in a group; they command more attention than others, whether they themselves welcome this or not. When such a feature is one that is generally considered by society to be an admirable one, the person who possesses it may easily confuse the part with the whole and regard themselves as superior. And society usually colludes with this error.

What of those who do not stand out, who have no exceptional features? They are unfortunate in that they are readily deemed to be ordinary in the corrupted sense of the word: dull, predictable, unimaginative, and uninteresting, the 9-to-5 commuter in the grey suit, the housewife whose horizons do not extend beyond cleaning the kitchen. We are all limited by the stereotypes of society, but this hazard applies equally to those of us who are prominent; the media star is severely confined not only by the conventions of the genre but by individual eccentricities that the public have taken to heart. It would seem that if we are to understand ordinariness, we need to recognize that richness of experience is not to be equated with special talents, competences, or arresting characteristics. If such a confusion were not so widespread, we would not be so easily persuaded to abandon wholeness in favor of competitiveness and glamor.

The confusion, however, is not simply a matter of logic but derives from the craving to be special. To be the preferred one and the center of attention is to have the illusion that we can evade the pain, disillusionment, and ultimate destination of ordinary living, an illusion that ignores the difference between the magic of imagination and the belief in a magic formula that enables us to escape our mortality.

THE CRAVING TO BE SPECIAL

In our society, there is a powerful conditioning factor that undermines our satisfaction with the ordinary. From an early age, we are encouraged to be special: to stand out from our contemporaries in some way or another, to be better, to excel, to beat the rest. This is most apparent in the field of education, where children are increasingly tested, evaluated, and given the impression that the chief aim of learning is to do better than others. This is not to deny the reasoning behind competition: if desirable jobs are scarce, then only those who excel in their examinations will get them. But the prestige that accompanies success in education or in other realms of endeavor far outstrips the practical aspects of the matter. Undergraduates do not kill themselves simply because they doubt whether they will get the most desirable job.

The desire to be special has been with us all throughout

history, and we cannot account for it exclusively in terms of contemporary society's particular attraction to specialness, technology, and the startling image. One way of understanding the phenomenon, the way most readily chosen by all those who have been influenced by Freud, is to focus on the child's early experience in the family, in particular his craving to enjoy the attention of his parents and to be preferred to his siblings. The force of this craving is brought home to us in the striking way it is so often repeated in the consulting room and by the havoc it can engender in the lives of certain disturbed people.

Main (1957) describes a series of patients met with in psychiatric hospital practice whom he terms *Special Patients*. The Special Patient (who is usually a woman) stimulates in her doctor or nurse a tendency to regard her as a unique case for which ordinary hospital practices are inappropriate and to engage in a secret relationship with her from which both parties derive satisfaction and a feeling of superiority over the rest of staff and patients. "The favourite nurse," writes Main

> came to believe from subtle remarks by the patient that the other nurses, good and effortful though they were, did not have the same deep understanding, so that she would become the patient's unspoken agent, ready to scheme against and control colleagues whose behaviour she felt, through no fault of their own, to be unsuitable for her patient. Increasingly the nurse concerned found herself irresistibly needed by the patient, and sometimes by the therapist, to take over increasing responsibility for some of the patient's ego-activities, to think for and decide for the patient . . . [p. 30]

The special privileges and attentions given to these patients, however, proved worthless: "Thus, during their stay in hospital these patients became Special, and particular individuals became worn out in the process of attending their needs. The patients, appealing at first, and suffering obviously, slowly became insatiable, and every effort to help them failed" (p. 31). Main describes these patients as searching for love using appealing and guilt-stimulating tactics; insatiability occurred because what was provoked to be given contained concealed hostility and thus increased the need for reassurance and love. He suggests that the condition is a form of addiction, the origin of which lies in the mother's failure to respond to the child's needs appropriately and her substituting a particular response (e.g., feeding) in a misguided attempt to satisfy him.

Another way of explaining this is to say that someone who has not been able to attain a sense of ordinariness compensates by seeking an exclusive, special relationship, first and foremost with the mother. In this case, he becomes unduly dependent on one particular relationship, and the qualities that would lead him to have confidence in himself are not his real qualities but only those that happen to have importance in one person's eyes. I shall now describe some features of a patient whose disturbance showed some similarity to Main's description. I have extracted this account from a paper I wrote in the early stages of my career (Lomas 1962, pp. 339–346). It is written with a kind of detached knowingness, characteristic of my work at that time, which makes me want to disown it. However, I cannot provide a better example, and it has the advantage that, with the passage of time, it becomes much easier to preserve the anonymity of the patient.

> Monica, a vivacious woman in her early thirties, came for treatment with a multiplicity of disabilities, many of them conversion symptoms such as pseudocyesis and transient paralysis of the limbs.
>
> She was financially dependent on her mother, and although lacking ready money to spend how she might choose she was in most ways well provided for. Her clothes

were obviously expensive and she drove to her sessions in a red sports car of which she was flamboyantly proud. Although, as she did no work, her time was potentially flexible, she found it very difficult to attend at the session times I offered her, did everything in her power to make me alter them, and felt terribly threatened by my refusal to do so.

When she first came for analysis she had a tumor in the neck region requiring operation but was too afraid to leave her mother and enter hospital where she would be "only a number, not a person," a situation which she feared would deprive her of her sense of reality and send her mad. It was not until she had suffered two more years of considerable pain that she decided to undergo this ordeal, and only then in the knowledge that she would be a private patient, that I would notify the surgeon about her mental state and that I and her general practitioner would visit her in hospital.

Her wish that I treat her as a special case is expressed in the following dream: "One day when I came for my session, your consulting room was furnished lavishly enough to receive a duchess. You were much more suave and elegant than you really are and looked like Rex Harrison [the film star]. 'So this is where you see your pet patients!' I said. Later in the dream, you turned into a homicidal maniac and were shot dead by the police." Associations to the dream linked me with her mother. One meaning of the dream would seem to be that she wished me to be the ideal mother to whom she was a special pet case, but such a situation was feared to be a false one covering up my hostility and dangerousness.

Monica's manifest illness originated at the age of 11, when the family moved to a new neighborhood and she attended a new school. She felt lonely, unbefriended and a misfit. She developed a transient hostility to her mother followed by an alarming fear that the Devil would take possession of her and take her away from her mother. Sometimes she fancied she could feel his breath on her pillow. The Devil was also identified with her new [male] school teacher who she feared might gain "more say over me than my mother." Since that time her mother had never been quite real to her and she desperately looked time and again at her mother's photograph to try to convince herself that it represented the same person who was still living with her. As an adult she remained emotionally tied to her mother to such an extent that she could not leave home even for a holiday, could not conceive of loving anyone else, and believed that when her mother died her own life would be finished also.

Monica had a way of looking at the world which shed light on these fears. People were divided into two classes: "family" and "strangers." "Family" would help one in trouble; "strangers" would leave one to die in the street. Although she came to me for help and gradually developed some trust in me it was a long time before she could feel, with any degree of conviction, that if she became ill when visiting me I would not leave her to die. There was a scale of increasing strangeness; from her mother, to the family, to her fellow-countrymen, and finally, foreigners.

This view of life, which tied Monica to her mother, was fostered by the latter, a lonely and aging widow. The mutual dependence became understandable when traced back to its origins. Her mother had been keen to have a child early in her marriage but remained sterile for ten years in spite of despairing visits to most of the eminent gynecologists in Europe. Finally, after a train of events that seemed to her almost miraculous, she conceived and a daughter was born. This long-awaited child died from tuberculosis at 18 months. Monica was born 3 years later and remained an only child. When she was 3 years old her father, who was a successful lawyer, died suddenly and unexpectedly as a result of a street accident, and her mother was prostrated with grief for a long time. Monica has been told that at the time she said to her mother: "Never mind, Mummy, I'll look after you now." It is not surprising that she became a spoilt child, a "poor, little rich girl" with many toys but few friends, whose whims were attended to but who had to be wrapped up in a mass of clothing even in the heat of summer. . . .

Monica felt that although her mother would help her and "do anything for her" she conveyed that these things were done because she was an unusually devoted mother who could patiently tolerate her daughter's whims and not because the daughter, Monica, really needed or deserved them. This state of affairs, although probably containing satisfactions to both parties, did not contribute to Monica's belief in herself and her sanity.

Monica certainly visualized her family as special. This idealization derived not only from her own defensive need to deny her hostility but from the picture of the family that had been painted by her mother and others. She described her parents as having made an ideal marriage. Everyone in the neighborhood agreed that both were exceptional people. Even now, people "worship" her mother and come to her for help and advice they can obtain nowhere else. She has only to say now, "I am Mr. E.'s [or Mrs. E.'s] daughter" and she will be respected and treated as a special person. She thinks of her father as standing out at the right hand of God, looking down on her. "If you are in trouble," her mother tells her, "look at the brightest star in the sky and that will be your father looking down on you, and he will take care of you"; and to this day Monica does so and takes comfort. But in the street or in a hospital ward, among strangers, Monica loses her sense of identity and becomes depersonalized. "Without my mother," she says, "I am nothing. There is nothing but a terrible emptiness. I even lose the picture of my mother in my mind."

It would seem that Monica, lacking the experience of being recognized as an individual, now depends on being known as a member of a particular group, the E. family. Value resides primarily in her father and mother and only secondarily in herself. Therefore, among strangers she does not really exist. And she cannot carry her picture of her mother with her because it cannot withstand the critical onslaught of strangers. She knows, really, that in failing to treat her as special, the strangers, by implication, destroy the myth of her parent's omnipotence. [pp. 340–342]

It was not only that she lacked an ability to form relationships because of the failure of her original relationship to her mother, but that the nonmother world had been presented to her in such a false light that she despaired of relating to it. Either it was a special place not governed by natural law but susceptible to her mother's magic or it was an alien and unfriendly realm unresponsive to real effort, inimicable to her needs, and lacking in understanding in them. Monica's sense of identity, based on the belief that her mother, and only her mother, could understand and tolerate the strange creature that she was, had validity only within the home.

The essential feature of Monica's predicament was that she had been forced into a position of passivity. She had been seduced into the acceptance of a special role which, however much she may have welcomed its benefits with a part of her mind, had nothing to do with her essential native potentialities which consequently atrophied. Ordinary activity, such as is required for normal living in a non-special set-up, was beyond her capacity, leaving her with the choice of helplessness or the adoption of a false personality the partial collapse of which led her to seek psychoanalysis.

The allocation of a special, but inauthentic, role in the family may induce the child to preserve, in secret, his or her uniqueness, and can be one of the factors contributing to the hidden true self described by Winnicott. Paradoxically, this may result in yet another assertion of being special. . . .

A hidden identity of this kind is more likely to make its appearance in the more secret symbolic world of artistic creativity than in the everyday world of human relationships. The artist is in many ways a special kind of person; in his sphere of creative activity he refuses to accept the ordinary standards and is sensitive and particular beyond all normal reason. In contrast to the 'Special Patient,' however, he is realistic enough in his particular field to accept the limitations of the material he has to work with and to apply self-criticism. He is sufficiently interested in a part of the world to want to approve it; but in the other aspects of his life this realistic attitude often fails him, and his sensitivity manifests itself in a sterile and egotistical dependence. [pp. 342–345]

THE VALUE OF ORDINARINESS

The craving to be ordinary, on the other hand, is exemplified by a woman who told me of the shame and misery she felt because her clothes were unlike those of her schoolmates. Her mother made them herself, and although she was skilled at doing so, the garments were old-fashioned and came down to her ankles. "If only," she said, "I could have gone into a shop and bought a pretty dress like the other girls."

I recount this memory not because it is unusual but because it is so common. There must be few of us who have not felt, as she did, the urgent wish to pass as an ordinary, acknowledged member of a group, who have not molded or disguised ourselves in order to be accepted without a questioning of our suitability to belong. The most fearsome example of this need is our craving to be recognized simply as an ordinary, sound human being. Those who suffer from an incapacitating mental disturbance often feel alienated from the human race, a pathological, subnormal, freakish phenomenon—and, indeed, this view of themselves is all too readily accentuated by the attitude of society. What then are we to make of the paradox that people have an urge to be both ordinary and special?

The infant, one imagines, is not at first caught in this fix. He needs to be recognized for what he is. He is neither ordinary nor special; he is himself. It is only when he begins to make comparisons with others that this kind of dilemma arises. In order not to lose his sense of identity, he needs to be confident of his uniqueness; yet it is clearly important to him that he be like others. If things go well, this paradox, like so many of the paradoxes that we have to live with, will be absorbed into his conception of himself without harm, and ordinary experience will provide enough richness, excitement, and security; however much the course of his life may bring adventure, drama, and success, he does not need them to replace an emptiness. The main reason why ordinariness does not satisfy someone is that he has not experienced enough meaning from his relationships to sustain a confidence in himself and in the possibilities of life.

It is ironic, inspiring, and sad that people are not uncommonly jolted into recognizing the value of ordinary living in the face of their impending death. Tolstoy's moving story "The Death of Ivan Illich" is a beautiful example of such a change of heart. An example from actual life is the description by Richard Neuberger shortly before his death from cancer (Yalom 1980):

> A change came over me which I believe is irreversible. Questions of prestige, of political success, of financial status, became all at once unimportant. In those first hours when I realized I had cancer, I never thought of my seat in the Senate, of my bank account, or of the destiny of the free world. . . . My wife and I have not had a quarrel since my illness was diagnosed. I used to scold her about squeezing the toothpaste from the top instead of the bottom, about not catering sufficiently to my fussy appetite, about making up guest lists without consulting me, about spending too much on clothes. Now I am either unaware of such matters, or they seem irrelevant. . . .
>
> In their stead has come a new appreciation of things I once took for granted—eating lunch with a friend, scratching Muffet's ears and listening for his purrs, the company of my wife, reading a book or magazine in the quiet cone of my bed lamp at night, raiding the refrigerator for a glass of orange juice or slice of coffee cake. For the first time I think I actually am savoring life. I realize, finally, that I am not immortal. I shudder when I remember all the occasions that I spoiled for myself—even when I was in the best of health—by false pride, synthetic values, and fancied slights. [p. 35]

THE MAKING OF A RELATIONSHIP

Because of the significance to emotional health of a sense of the ordinary, it is important to consider the ways in which our attitude to the patient may, or may not, help to cultivate it.

When faced with the desperate plea by a patient that we assuage his misery, it is perhaps understandable, as I have suggested earlier, that the therapist might feel the need of special power and may fail to recognize that his success or failure depends in no small part on the same human capacities that are called upon in his nonprofessional relationships; and that, if these are lacking, no amount of theory, technique, or experience will rescue him. It may be thought that in presenting this view of psychotherapy I am unwittingly making a claim for it to be rather a *special* undertaking requiring outstanding personal attributes. But this is not the case. There are many undertakings in life that call (perhaps in vain) for outstanding personal attributes, and we can meet these requirements only to the extent that our limitations allow.

One confusion to which I refer in my earlier discussion of the subject (Chapter 9) is that the psychotherapist takes on a role that, in some ways, possesses more of a resemblance to acting than do many occupations. This is not to say that acting is not an ordinary pursuit. One does, however, need to make a clear distinction between the actor herself and the character she is impersonating in the play. The psychotherapist, because of the degree to which she suppresses her individual personality and encourages fantasy, may readily feel and be felt to be an actor in a drama. In other words, she may play her part with such conviction that she loses her sense of ordinary living. If, however, it is the case that the patient needs to accept his ordinariness, then it would seem important that the therapist behave in as ordinary a way as circumstances permit, and that she avoid the confusions that result from a faulty conception of psychotherapy or personal narcissism or both.

Recently, I was talking to a colleague who felt that her spontaneity with patients was eroded by her stereotyped, habitual way of being with them from the moment she opened the door of her consulting room. She did not use the word *ordinary*, but I think that her unease could be put in terms of her inability (which she by no means considered to be uncommon) to be herself with her patients. Why should this be so difficult? Even those of us who do not adhere to orthodox psychoanalytic technique find it hard not to behave with a rigidity that we would prefer to shed. We appear to need to present ourselves as special, as beings above and immune to the pettiness and scratchiness of ordinary mortals.

By an odd coincidence, shortly after writing the above paragraph, something occurred that seemed to bear out my colleague's comments. I phoned a patient to discuss a forth-coming change of session time. I had taken a week off work to paint my room, get some writing done, and catch up with various tasks. It was now the end of the week. During our conversation, the patient broke off to say: "What's happened to you? You sound quite different—so friendly and relaxed. It's not that you're rude in sessions, but you're reserved and predictable. Now you're all over the place, and it's great to talk to you. Why is it? Do you get bogged down at work?"

My patient's spontaneous and unexpected exclamations gave me food for thought. Unhappily, I think she is right. At work I find myself easily falling into a routinized and relatively restrained way of being. I believe also that (despite any theories that might support the opposite view) it would be better for my patients if I were able to be more like I had been on this particular occasion.

It can be legitimately argued that some of our patients need us to be godlike some of the time. But the persistence with which we preserve our specialness cannot, I believe, be fully accounted for by this consideration. The relief, and even warmth, that so often is the response of patients who, often by accident, light upon my humanness is impressive. If I unwittingly reveal an idiosyncrasy or make a simple mistake, or it is discovered that I do the same sort of things that other people do (if, for example, a patient sees me in the middle of an action that I am doing without noticeable skill or enjoyment), patients are more likely to take comfort from the observation rather than be disturbed by it. They discover with their own eyes (for telling them about myself doesn't seem to have a comparable impact) that, after all, I am an ordinary person. What is significant is that, far from providing a catastrophic disillusionment, such revelations usually improve matters. I conclude, therefore, that our assiduous, and largely unconscious, attempts to appear special have less rational roots; they are a function of a personal narcissism that is enhanced by the vanities of our profession. In our defense, we can make the plea that psychotherapy is a lonely job in which our own emotional needs are subdued in the service of the patient, that we are often lost and insecure, and that it is understandable if we compensate by taking an undue pride in a responsible and caring stance. But perhaps it would be better if we compensated by eating cream cakes. If disturbed people have a craving to feel and be accepted by their fellows as a similar being and lack the capacity to enjoy the simple experiences of life—feeling, thinking, looking, eating, sleeping, mating, and so on—then the function of the therapist is to help them to attain this state. It would therefore seem appropriate not only to explore the reasons for such disabilities but to present an atmosphere in the consulting room likely to encourage and cultivate the simple qualities that the patient lacks. If we are to accomplish this task, we must look carefully at the kind of relationship we foster and our ways of achieving this.

The traditional aim of psychoanalysis is to observe, understand, and communicate the understanding in an atmosphere in which the patient feels safe. There is no mention of friendship or intimacy. A colleague of mine—a psychoanalyst whose thoughts and writings I admire—once said to me, "I do not try to get to know my patients." I believe, however, that if we are to bring a semblance of ordinariness into the consulting room, we must aim to get to know our patients, much as two people meeting in daily living usually aim to know each other in a mutually exploratory way. Should one of the participants insist, and have his insistence accepted, that the conversation be conducted exclusively in terms of his own particular ideology—say, Christianity or dialectic materialism—the atmosphere will be such that the two people will not be well placed to get to know each other.

The reader may well think that I am losing sight of the fact that in many situations in life the functional aim of the relationship transcends or contravenes the natural wish for intimacy; and so it may be in many cases (although considerably less so, I believe, than is commonly supposed). That psychotherapy should be included in this category is a view, however, that I would want to debate.

Why does the patient wish to know and be known? Why does he dream of everyday, intimate relationships with his therapist? The answer the therapist is most likely to give is that he craves the love of an idealized and relatively unavailable parent; in short, it is a manifestation of transference. But is there more to it than this?

The intense desire for a more ordinary relationship stems in no small part from the sheer deprivation and humiliation experienced in coming for therapy. The professional reserve and formality of the therapist is acutely painful, accentuating the necessary inequality of need and provoking a comparable lack of spontaneity in a situation in which his expressions will be translated into another and apparently superior tongue rather then simply received as something given.

There is, moreover, the matter of trust. We may accept a

viewpoint because of our faith in its source; it is proclaimed by someone who has prestige. Alternatively, we may wish to know as much as possible about the reasons for the viewpoint, the evidence on which it is based, and the philosophical and emotional stance of the speaker. In the realm of psychotherapy, the former trust is rather akin to that of suggestion or hypnosis. In the latter, it is based on knowing the reasoning, and possible bias, of the person concerned. The kind of trust that is appropriate to long-term therapy and that gives maximum autonomy to the patient is, I believe, the latter. The more the patient knows us—our experience of living, our training, our idiosyncrasies, and limitations—the better position he is in to assess our words, the greater his confidence that we are not trying to brainwash him, and the more light he himself can bring to the discussion.

In view of these considerations, it may be useful to conceive of psychotherapy as an attempt, on both sides, to make a relationship. As the patient has failed, in one way or another, to make satisfactory relationships, this would seem to be a legitimate and even necessary aim; and, indeed, psychotherapists often recognize this fact even if they do not overtly declare it to be so or take it as a paradigm of their work. What I am suggesting, therefore, is that the therapist should not content herself with interpreting the defenses that stand in the way of intimacy or even with adopting a receptive stance to the patient, but that she should take the responsibility of getting to know him. And this means that she cannot depart too radically from the ways of getting to know people in other situations: the tentative, risky, tactful, revealing, confronting, and innumerable other attitudes that go along the path to intimacy. It is in the movement of a free and open relationship that changes and that converts possibilities into actualities that we best see others, including the rough-and-tumble that go with passion and the

light-heartedness that comes from informality. We cannot always make this happen; we can only try. Often we do not know
what has made it possible. A colleague told me yesterday, with
some bewilderment, how at ease she feels with a certain very sick
patient. "I can cry in his presence," she said, "and it is rare for me
to cry before anybody." Significantly she added, "Actually, the
therapy is going very well."

I do not wish to underestimate the difficulties that face the
therapist who hopes to make as ordinary a relationship with her
patient as she can, for she has the responsibility of safe-guarding
him from traumatic experiences and must therefore be willing to
restrain her own desires. But this is, I believe, a limitation to be
transcended as much as possible rather than increased by excessive caution.

According to Ernest Gellner (1992), psychoanalysis is a
form of mysticism, a phenomenon defined by him as "an intense
emotional experience, which at the same time purports to be
and is felt as being the acquisition of knowledge which is
important, privileged and out of the ordinary" (p. 41). In psychoanalysis, qualified masters are endowed with a special technique by means of which they can enlighten followers in a
luminous experience that is its own validation. Freud created a
theory that enabled this mystical experience to be regarded,
unlike other mysticisms, as part of the natural world, thus
making it more acceptable to contemporary thought. The need
now, I believe, is to demystify the practice of psychotherapy and
to recognize that the experiences within it not only are part of
the natural world but can be encompassed by our ordinary
capacities for experience.

Chapter Fourteen

The Principles of Teaching Psychotherapy

A man may have discovered some portion of truth or wisdom, after spending a great deal of time and trouble in thinking it over for himself and adding thought to thought; and it may sometimes happen that he could have found it all ready to hand in a book and spared himself the trouble. But even so, it is a hundred times more valuable if he has acquired it by thinking it out for himself.

—Arthur Schopenhauer

Because there is so little agreement about the nature of psychotherapy, the teaching of it is problematic. In this book, I have suggested that, in the broadest terms, psychotherapy is an attempt to effect a beneficial change on another by means of a personal relationship.

This statement begs all kinds of questions, for what is beneficial depends on how we think people should live. Most psychotherapists would, I believe, assert that people live most richly when they have autonomy of experience—when they are as free as possible from inner contradictions and external impingements. It would seem, therefore, that students should be helped to recognize and understand the ways in which people restrict themselves, how this comes about, and the appropriate measures that can be taken to free them from such bondage. The most important factors in the therapist's ability to make an impact on these restrictions are an intuitive understanding of others, a preparedness to engage them with hope and openness, and an ability to influence that is based on encouragement rather than command. The intuition that a student brings to his apprenticeship (the recognition of which is crucial to good selection) can be augmented by personal therapy and any other measures that enable him to deepen his experience of those who come to him for help. These measures will include discussion of his work with others and access to the ideas of those who have been creative in the field.

SELECTION OF STUDENTS

One of the most important features of any training scheme is the criteria used for selection of candidate. Because of the high status accorded to academic prowess, a university degree is often regarded as essential, particularly if it has been gained in a subject that has some relevance to the study of people, for example, medicine or psychology. There are, of course, many areas of learning that have a bearing on the practice of psychotherapy. Hobson (1985), for example, recommends the study of Shakespeare and the authorized version of the Bible; and, indeed, many therapists believe that poets and novelists have more to teach about the nature of relationships than does psychology, let alone medicine. It would seem, therefore, that the recommended area of study is too narrow. To have achieved a degree in any subject does, at least, show that the candidate has some competence in getting to grips with a subject. We should not, however, let ourselves be too impressed by this. The capacity to learn theory or to write essays has little connection with the ability to help people in distress. The latter is best learned in ordinary life, and the people that are most fitted to do the work are those who have a burning curiosity in the wishes, feelings, and thoughts of others and an interest in their well-being. I am reminded of Socrates' reply when asked his city of origin: "I am a citizen of the world."

CULTIVATING INTUITION

I have suggested in this book that a crucial element in successful therapy is that the patient should perceive his helper to be genuine—to mean what he says and to show by his gestures, tone of voice, and general manner that he is not acting a part. This does not imply that the patient would necessarily be disconcerted to find that the therapist followed certain lines of thought derived from his experience and training, but that such thinking should not cause him to be false, to stray far from a truthful presentation of himself. In other words, in good therapy, the patient experiences a personal style, one that is not cramped by doctrine. If this be so, a good training is one that allows and encourages the student to trust, as far as possible, his own intuitive capacity and to build on his own style of being with people rather than suppressing it and replacing it with a formula for behavior imposed from without.

To show the student, in a constructive manner, the ways in which the existent blocks in his perception and his limitation of experience detract from his efficacy is a delicate task. The criteria for making a useful response to a patient are not hard and fast, and it is easy to swamp or mislead a student with a babel of interpretations that undermine his confidence—an occurrence that can happen all too often in group seminars in which competitiveness and envy flourish.

To create an atmosphere of justified trust in the goodwill of others—whether fellow students or teachers—is no easy task. If I could present a formula for doing so, I would no doubt become a hero overnight. But a training scheme based on the recognition that students are mature people capable of learning from each other and participating fully in the organization of their learning program may help toward this goal. The teacher in this case would be seen as someone willing to not only give his impressions of the student's ideas and ways of working but share openly his own experience, including his doubts and mistakes.

The dividing line between the kind of observation that is releasing and that which is restricting is a narrow one. In the former case, the student feels that his right to autonomy is sacrosanct, and his position is a safe one despite whatever criticisms the teacher may have. He is not under threat of complete rejection; he may assert his own viewpoint without serious retaliation (although not necessarily avoiding painful confrontation). His position is similar to that of the patient in therapy, except that he takes on more responsibility for his own words and actions in the room.

THE HAZARDS OF SCRUTINY

One factor that may lead a student to feel unduly constricted is the level of intensity of the scrutiny. We live in an intrusive society, one in which the amount of inspection and monitoring of its members is unparalleled and increasing, and the practice of therapy does not escape this influence. Undue watchfulness and overprotection have, as we know, a baleful effect on the growth of a child. It is natural and healthy for a parent to watch her child, to observe him with curiosity, wonder, love, and concern for his safety. But when, because of narcissistic preoccupation, fear of projected impulses, ideals of perfection, paranoid fear of impurities from without, or apprehension of the opinions of friends and neighbors, the control is excessive, the child has no space to explore, play, test, and live with the ambiguities that are necessary for creativity.

This kind of situation has both similarities and differences to that of learning psychotherapy. It is similar in that the development that is relevant is more akin to the growth of a person as a whole than to, say, the technical ability to work a computer. It is different in that the student is not a child in need of a parent but an adult who needs another person of comparable stature and status but more experienced in his particular field of study. This paradoxical and unusual relationship is not an easy one to negotiate.

To the extent that a teacher of a training organization is concerned with judging the capacity of a student to practice psychotherapy and to empowering him to do so, we are in another ball game. There is a world of difference between the feedback that implies "Perhaps I can help you to do this better" or "I'm wondering if you are fit to practice, now or ever." The latter statement is liable, to a damaging extent, to restrict creativity, and in view of what has been said above, is dangerously inhibiting.

The ways in which power can insidiously guide and restrict the kinds of discourse that seem possible to us have been cogently documented. Taking sexuality as one example of many, Michael Foucault (1979) concludes that, far from freeing it from the bonds of Victorian morality, we now have more effective means of controlling it:

> It may be the case that the intervention of the Church in conjugal sexuality and its rejection of "frauds" against procreation had lost much of their insistence over the previous two hundred years. But medicine made a forceful entry into the pleasures of the couple: it created an entire organic functional or mental pathology arising out of "incomplete" sexual practices; it carefully classified all forms of related pleasures; it incorporated them into the notions of "development" and instinctual "disturbances"; and it undertook to manage them. [p. 41]

Foucault also refers to "the pleasure that comes from exercising a power that questions, monitors, watches, spies, searches out, palpates, brings to light" and, on the other hand, "the pleasure that kindles at having to evade this power, flee from it, tool it, or travesty it" (p. 45). If Foucault is right, we are indeed in a fix at the present time, and much of our potentially creative energy for learning and practicing is being dissipated.

THE REGISTRATION OF PSYCHOTHERAPISTS

The graduation of students by an organization that is accepted by the professional world is an understandable wish. By its means, the prospective patient's fears that he may fall into the hands of an immoral and incompetent practitioner are lessened. Although this is a gain, it is not such an unambiguous one as appears at first sight, for not only, alas, can it lead to a false sense of trust in the practitioner's integrity and ability, but it tends to deprive the public of those approaches that lie outside the often narrow parameters of the profession in question.

In a profession such as medicine, in which the monitoring of results by scientific technique is possible in many areas, the justification for graduation and registration carries some conviction despite the telling criticism of Illich (1976) and others. The case of registration in psychotherapy is another matter, for it is not a science and cannot be satisfactorily formulated in quantitative terms. It is a unique undertaking and does not fall into a category other than its own. If, however, one were to choose between science and art as a home for psychotherapy, one would probably do better to select the latter. Just as there is little general consensus as to what constitutes good contemporary art, so there is little agreement at present among psychotherapists about the theory and the practice of their work. The product of the artist cannot be quantified. The time taken at art college is little guide to future accomplishment, and there are superlative practitioners who have never seen the inside of an art college. The parallel does not of course entirely work, for the artist's production can at least be viewed by the public (even if the public does not know what to make of it). And individual recipients, except perhaps models, do not have to be protected from his work, provided that he is not regarded as a subversive threat to established society and a corrupter of the morals of its members. These problems should give us pause before assuming that the organization of the profession of psychotherapists should be based on that of doctors and dentists.

The dilemma about granting professional respectability to a student or organization of psychotherapy is attributable, I believe, not only to the misunderstandings about the nature of the work (which I discuss here) but to a peculiar kind of caution that is endemic to our society. Policies—and mistakes—which result in undramatic limitations of potentiality for benefiting others are regarded as acceptable, for the system can still appear to be controlled and the limitations can be rationalized. But mistakes that manifest themselves with more immediacy and are the result of human error are pursued with obsessional zeal and a mistaken belief that such errors can be avoided by ever-increasing rules, regulations, and discipline. This tendency is manifested in the field of psychotherapy in Britain in the way in which the profession has attempted to form a Register of therapists. I do not propose to describe here this debacle, the details of which are familiar to members of the profession. What is notable is that, although there exist many therapists who, like myself, value freedom of method, discussions have unfortunately resulted in an inexorable progress toward a restrictive code of practice. A formula for all training organizations based on criteria that are simple to set down on paper, are quantitative rather than qualitative, and give the appearance of rigor and caution is seductively attractive to many. The consequence, I believe, will be an erosion of spontaneity, a dampening of creativity, and a feeble conformity in which the vitality of psychotherapy will survive only with difficulty. This is too high a price to pay. Ideally, it should be possible to create a register that is not so debilitating, but given the mood of obsessional control and the clamor for even more prestige, this aim appears to be beyond our grasp. Perhaps we should put more effort into enlightening the public, as best we can, about the nature of psychotherapy and providing easier access to information that would enable people to choose a good therapist.

I do not believe, however, that the adventure that Freud began will dissipate so easily. The experiences that occur in the consulting room are so powerful, so rich, so moving, and sometimes so creative that those who participate in the endeavor are unlikely to allow the whole thing to evaporate in the face of rules and regulations.

I am encouraged in this view by my contact with students over the past few years, especially a number who have joined together in Cambridge to form a student-oriented training scheme. Elsewhere (Lomas 1990), I have described the early stages of the formation of this group. Briefly, it is an attempt to establish a set-up in which students, both as a group and as individuals, have as much autonomy as possible and in which they have an opportunity to develop their own approach to their task, in their own way and their own time, rather than having a structured course imposed upon them.

We have now moved some way since my article about the group, and inevitably, as we grew in numbers, more organization became necessary (if only to save time and energy) with an inevitable loss of flexibility. However, by far the greatest obstacle to the maintenance of our ideals has been the need to modify our practice in order to be accepted by the register of psychotherapeutic training schemes. Nevertheless, much of the original philosophy and practice remains. The encouraging aspect of this is to have seen that, given this freedom and despite all the problems we have encountered, students have been able, with the help of more experienced practitioners, to organize a training scheme according to their beliefs and to have turned themselves into psychotherapists who have their own individual style and vision. The group, as the reader will guess, does not work in a Garden of Eden, but it reveals the potential in many of those who turn to this profession to cultivate their own gifts if given the freedom to do so.

References

Balint, M. (1968). *The Basic Fault*. London: Tavistock.

Bateson, G. (1973). *Steps to an Ecology of Mind*. St. Albans, NY: Paladin.

Bettelheim, B. (1983). Scandal in the family. *New York Review of Books*, June 30.

———— (1992). *Recollections and Reflections*. London: Penguin.

Binswanger, L. (1963). *Being in the World*. New York: Basic Books.

Boss, M. (1963). *Psychoanalysis and Daseinsanalysis*. New York: Basic Books.

Buber, M. (1961). *Between Man and Man*. London: Collins.

Casement, P. (1985). *On Learning from the Patient*. London: Tavistock.

Chabot, B. (1979). The right to care for each other and its silent erosion. *Tijdschrift Voor Psychotherapis* 5:199. (Published in Dutch).

Douglas, M. (1975). *Implicit Meanings: Essays in Anthropology*. London: Routledge and Kegan Paul.

Ellenberger, H. F. (1970). *The Discovery of the Unconscious*. London: Penguin.

Erickson, E. (1968). *Identity: Youth and Crisis*. London: Faber.

Fairbairn, W. R. D. (1952). *Psychoanalytical Studies of the Personality*. London: Tavistock.

Farber, L. (1976). *Lying, Despair, Jealously, Envy, Sex, Suicide, Drugs and the Good Life*. New York: Basic Books.

Fenichel, O. (1946). *The Psychoanalytic Theory of Neurosis*. London: Routledge and Kegan Paul.

Ferenczi, S. (1988). *The Clinical Diary of Sandor Ferenczi*. Ed. J. Dupont. Trans. M. Balint and N. Z. Jackson. Cambridge, MA: Harvard University Press.

Forrester, J. (1990). *The Seductions of Psychoanalysis: Freud, Lacan, and Derrida*. Cambridge, England: Cambridge University Press.

Foucault, M. (1979). *The History of Sexuality*. Vol. 1: *An Introduction*. London: Allen Lane.

Freud, S. (1913). On beginning the treatment. *Standard Edition* 12:123. London: Hogarth, 1958.

Fromm, E. (1951). *The Forgotten Language: An Introduction to the Understanding of Dreams, Myths and Fairytales*. New York: Holt, Reinhart and Winston.

Gellner, E. (1992). Psychoanalysis, social role and testability. In *Psychotherapy and its Discontents*, ed. W. Dryden and C. Feltham, p. 41. Buckingham, England: Open University Press.

Goffman, E. (1975). *Frame Analysis*. London: Penguin.

Guntrip, H. (1968). *Schizoid Phenomena Object Relations and the Self*. London: Hogarth.

Halmos, P. (1965). *The Faith of the Counsellors*. London: Constable.

Hampshire, S. (1989). *Innocence and Experience*. London. Penguin.

Hayley, T. (1990). Charisma, psychoanalysts, medicine-man and metaphor. *International Review of Psycho-Analysis* 17:1.

Hobson, R. (1985). *Forms of Feeling*. London: Tavistock.

Hoffer, A. (1991). The Freud-Ferenczi Controversy—a living legacy. *International Review of Psycho-Analysis* 18:465.

Illich, I. (1976). *Limits to Medicine*. London: Marion Boyars.

Klauber, J. (1987). *Illusion and Spontaneity in Psychoanalysis*. London: Free Association.

Klein, M. (1932). *The Psychoanalysis of Children*. London: Hogarth.

Kuhn, T. (1970). *The Structure of Scientific Revolutions*. Chicago: University of Chicago Press.

Lacan, J. (1988). *The Seminar*. Book 1: *Freud's Papers on Technique, 1953–1954*. Trans. with notes by J. Forrester. Cambridge, England: Cambridge University Press.

Laing, R. D. (1960). *The Divided Self*. London: Tavistock.

Langs, R. J. (1985). *The Listening Process*. New York: Jason Aronson.

Levi-Strauss, C. (1968). *Structural Anthropology*. London: Penguin.

Lomas, P. (1973). *True and False Experience*. London: Allen Lane.

———— (1981). *The Case for a Personal Psychotherapy*. Oxford, England: Oxford University Press. Republished under the title *The Psychotherapy of Everyday Life*. New Brunswick: Transaction, 1993.

———— (1987). *The Limits of Interpretation*. London: Penguin.

———— (1990). On setting up a psychotherapy training scheme. *Free Associations* 20:139. London: Free Association Books.

MacMurray, J. (1957). *The Self as Agent*. London: Faber.

Main, T. (1957). *British Journal of Medical Psychology* 30:129 Republished in *The Ailment and Other Psychoanalytic Essays*. London: Free Association Press 1989.

Miller, A. (1983). *For Your Own Good: Hidden Cruelty in Child-Rearing and the Roots of Violence*. Trans. Hildegard & Hunter. New York: Hannum, Farrar, Strauss, and Giroux.

Milner, M. (1969). *The Hands of the Living God*. London: Hogarth.

Murdoch, I. (1970). *The Sovereignty of Good*. Routledge and Kegan Paul.

Natterson, J. (1991). *Beyond Countertransference*. Northvale, NJ: Jason Aronson.

Park, J. (1992). *Shrinks: The Analysts Analyzed*. London: Bloomsbury.

Polyani, M. (1958). *Personal Knowledge*. London: Routledge and Kegan Paul.

Roazen, P. (1975). *Freud and His Followers*. New York: Knopf.

———— (1990). *The Clinical Diary of Sandor Ferenczi*. *American Journal of Psychoanalysis* 50:370.

Rycroft, C. (1972). *A Critical Dictionary of Psychoanalysis*. London: Penguin.

Schafer, R. (1976). *A New Language for Psychoanalysis*. New Haven, CT: Yale University Press.

———— (1983). *The Analytic Attitude*. London: Hogarth.

Searles, H. (1965). *Schizophrenia and Related Subjects*. London: Hogarth.

Spence, D. (1982). *Narrative Truth and Historical Truth*. New York: W. W. Norton.

_____ (1987). *The Freudian Metaphor*. New York: Norton.

Suttie, I. (1988). *The Origins of Love and Hate*. London: Free Associations Press.

Symington, N. (1990). The possibility of human freedom and its transmission (with particular reference to the thought of Bion). *International Journal of Psycho-Analysis* 71:101.

Tillich, P. (1952). *The Courage to Be*. London: Nisbet.

Winnicott, D. W. (1987). *Collected Papers: Through Paediatrics to Psychoanalysis*. London: Tavistock.

_____ (1987). *The Spontaneous Gesture: Selected Letters of D. W. Winnicott*. Ed. R. Rodman. Cambridge, MA: Harvard University Press.

Yalom, I. D. (1980). *Existential Psychotherapy*. New York: Basic Books.

Credits

The author gratefully acknowledges permission to reprint the following:

"The Origin of the Need to Be Special," by Peter Lomas, originally published in the *British Journal of Medical Psychology*, vol. 35, pp. 339–346. Copyright © 1962 by the *British Journal of Medical Psychology* and reprinted with permission of the journal.

"Days," by Philip Larkin. In *The Whitsun Weddings*. Copyright © 1964 by the estate of Philip Larkin. Reprinted by permission of Faber and Faber Inc.

Extract from "The Cool Web," by Robert Graves. In *Collected Poems*. Copyright © 1975 by A. P. Watts Ltd. on behalf of the trustees of the Robert Graves Copyright Trust. Reprinted by permission of Cassell and Co. and Oxford University Press.

Extract from "Let It Go," by William Empson. In *Collected Poems*. Copyright © 1949 by Chatto and Windus. Reprinted by permission of Harcourt Brace Jovanovich and the estate of the author.

Index

Absolute dependence, 102
Abstinence, 56–57, 106
Acting out, 76
Action language, 169
Ambiguity, reality development
    and, 126–127
Analytic attitude. *See also*
    Responsibility
    abstinence and, 56–57
    guilt and, 40
    merit of, 39–42
    spontaneity and, 42–46
Anguish
    diagnostic issues and, 89–98
    Freud's theory of
        psychopathology and
        critiques of, 85–89

dehumanizing aspects of, 85
therapeutic disadvantages
    of, 85–86
negative features of, 82–83
unnecessary terms for
    conceptualizing, 81–82

Balint, M., 111
Basic rule, 37–38
    reality of psychotherapy and,
        166–170
Bateson, G., 126
Bettelheim, B., 144–145
Binswanger, L., 86
Boss, M., 86
British object relations school, 7
Buber, M., 86